# THE BEST OF JOSEPH NICOLOSI

# THE BEST OF JOSEPH NICOLOSI

## Collected Articles *by* The Originator of Reparative Therapy®

JOSEPH NICOLOSI, Ph.D.

LIBERAL MIND PUBLISHERS

*Tarzana, California*

**The Best of Joseph Nicolosi: Collected Articles by the Originator of Reparative Therapy®**

First edition, with a Foreword, two articles and Conclusion, by Linda A. Nicolosi; with two Case Stories by David Pickup, M.A., LMFT


Published in the United States of America by
Liberal Mind Publishers,
PO Box 572859, Tarzana, CA 91357



**Library of Congress Cataloging-in-Publication Data:**
Nicolosi, Joseph, Ph.D.
The Best of Joseph Nicolosi, Ph.D.: Collected Articles
by the Originator of Reparative Therapy®
Foreword by Linda A. Nicolosi, with two Case Stories by David Pickup, M.A., LMFT
Bibliographical References

ISBN 978-0-9976373-8-0

1. Gay men—Mental health
2. Psychotherapy
3. Group psychotherapy
4. Homosexuality, male

The paper used in this publication meets the minimum requirements of American National Standard of Information Sciences—Permanence of Paper for Printed Library Materials. ANSI/NISO Z39.48-1992.

# Table of Contents

# THE BEST OF JOSEPH NICOLOSI

Collected Articles

*by*

The Originator of

Reparative Therapy®

JOSEPH NICOLOSI, PH.D.

# Foreword

*by Linda Ames Nicolosi*

On March 8, 2017, psychologist Dr. Joseph Nicolosi, Sr., my beloved husband of 39 years, died unexpectedly at the age of seventy.

On his gravestone is written this inscription: "Joseph Nicolosi, Ph.D.: *Warrior for Truth.*"

Always a dynamo of energy, Dr. Nicolosi had no idea that his time was short. His specialty had been treating men who sought to diminish their homosexuality and develop their heterosexual potential. At the time of his death, he was working on another book to retrieve some of the forgotten psychoanalytic studies on homosexuality.

During his 40-year career, he worked alongside more than 1,000 clients with unwanted same-sex attractions—more men, perhaps, than any other therapist in psychotherapeutic history.

As Clinical Director of the Thomas Aquinas Psychological Clinic, he also oversaw thousands more cases of men who were under the care of the therapists on his staff.

## Trailblazer

Dr. Nicolosi refused to be carried along by the culture-driven trends in his profession. The guiding principle that "normality is that which functions in accordance with its design" had once been unquestioned in his profession. But psychologists were gradually abandoning that view. *Design? Purpose? Nature?* Who spoke any more of those principles? Homosexuality had always been seen as a psychological problem; now it was viewed as an unchangeable and utterly inevitable *identity.*

Further, during his career, psychologists had turned over the "guarding of the henhouse to the foxes" — that is, they had relinquished control of the study of homosexuality to gay activists, the foxes, themselves. Prevented from acknowledging the family factors in the backgrounds of their homosexual clients, most mainstream psychologists were intimidated into a submissive silence.

My husband often lamented that so many of his colleagues (some of them particularly prominent in the profession) would profess agreement with him in private; however, only a few were willing to say so publicly. To be linked to reparative therapy was career suicide, as it carried with it the dreaded label of "anti-gay" or "homophobic."

There is a steep career cost to be paid by anyone who disagrees with the gay lobby, and with so many good men doing nothing, it was clear that evil—in the form of professional silence and intellectual dishonesty—would, for the time being, prevail. Undeterred, Dr. Nicolosi continued to promote the classic understanding of homosexuality as an attachment loss rooted in gender-based trauma.

The media and some of Dr. Nicolosi's colleagues mistook such a concept for quackery. They clumsily lumped reparative therapy into the vague and ominous-sounding category of "conversion therapy" which purportedly "converts" clients through shame-inducing coercion.

Shortly after Dr. Nicolosi's death, however, the United States Patent and Trademark Office identified "Reparative Therapy" by name as a distinct and separate mental-health therapy originated by Dr. Nicolosi, which employs evidence-based treatment interventions, and is not a mere form of "conversion therapy" per se.

The Thomas Aquinas Clinic had been completing a long-term outcome study of the progress of clients at the clinic. Dr. Nicolosi made a presentation of that data, "Clinical Outcomes for Same-Sex Attraction Distress: Change and Well-Being," with Carolyn Pela, Ph.D. at the Christian Association for Psychological Studies (CAPS) Conference in California in 2016.

## Change as an Ongoing Process

Dr. Nicolosi didn't "try" to change his clients' sexual orientation. In fact, sexuality was not a frequent topic of discussion in his sessions. Instead, by using established interventions, he treated the underlying gender trauma and behavioral addictions, after which clients would commonly notice decreases in their unwanted same-sex attractions and a new openness to opposite-sex feelings.

As with almost all psychological conditions treated in psychotherapy, however, complete change was not a common therapeutic outcome. Most clients reported satisfying changes which helped them understand the source of their conflicts, releasing them from compulsive sexual acting-out and giving them the tools to move on productively with their lives in a way that was consistent with their deeply held values. One could say that they learned how to "reintegrate" their true, masculine selves instead of eroticizing that masculine self in another man.

Many marriages were saved, as men learned that they didn't have to divorce their wives and claim a gay identity in order to be true to themselves. Addictions to gay porn were overcome, and some clients who never believed they would be able to marry, were able to do so when they learned how to satisfy their ongoing male affectional needs in a non-erotic way. On my husband's desk were many appreciative letters and photos from men who had gone on to marry and to have families.

Members of the clergy—priests, ministers, rabbis—were enabled to understand their same-sex erotic feelings, and to integrate them through a self-compassionate understanding so they could stay true to their vows. Confused teenagers who couldn't understand their crushes on other boys gained a new perspective on the meaning of those desires, and realized they didn't have to be gay. Men who had been sexually abused were freed from the compulsive need to reenact their childhood trauma with another male.

Dr. Nicolosi published four books in his lifetime: *Reparative Therapy of Male Homosexuality; Case Stories of Reparative Therapy*® (originally published as *Healing Homosexuality); A Parent's Guide to Preventing Homosexuality;* and *Shame and Attachment Loss: The Practical Work of Reparative Therapy.*

These books have been translated into Arabic, Bulgarian, Italian, Turkish, Polish, Romanian, Portuguese, German, Spanish, and Ukrainian, with articles appearing in Vietnamese, Chinese, Russian, and Hebrew.

## Is Homosexuality in Accord with Our Nature?

Dr. Nicolosi found himself increasingly alone in his profession. In today's culture, the idea that we "have a human nature"—other than that which we "design" or choose for ourselves—is fading from cultural consciousness. But for most people, I believe, the truth still lingers just under conscious awareness. When Joe and I sat together around the breakfast table, he would sometimes tell me, speaking of gay activists, "They lie."

"Really?" I would respond (I was always the one to try to avoid cynicism). "How can you say that?"

"To defend a lie," he would say, "you have to lie. A person can't legitimately claim an identity that's contrary to his design. And on some deep level, *they all know this*."

He meant that no one can simply erase the knowledge of what has shaped him; and no man can deny that he has a destiny to claim his maleness. Homosexuality is, he taught, a psychological condition that develops, like all psychological conditions, through a combination of early environment, later life-experiences, and, for some people, an element of biological predisposition. We often hear the media ask, "Is homosexuality a choice, or are people born that way?" This is as silly as asking, "Is depression a choice, or are people born that way?" "Gay" is not simply "who we are;" it is a chosen identity based on an *unchosen* way of experiencing the world—particularly gender.

The boy who develops homosexually is blameless—he is just an innocent child. But when he makes the decision to enter into a gay lifestyle, he has chosen to pay a terrible price. His understanding of gender will be sadly distorted, and he will cut himself off from healthy, authentic intimacy with a woman. Nature has, with her own stern finality, decreed that the gay man will never be able to have a biological child with his partner. The children that the gay couple brings into this world (through the help of a surrogate) will be purposely separated from the love and influence of their natural mother. Further, in sexual intimacy, the gay man abuses his body through unnatural anal and oral intercourse, and diminishes his God-given dignity as a man.

## The Most Common Childhood Pattern

Most of Dr. Nicolosi's clients described patterns of childhood experiences that were strikingly similar. Distilled into general terms, with some exceptions, of course, their story is as follows:

When boys reach the age of two-and-a-half (the gender-identity phase of development), they typically detach from their primary caregiver, who is the mother, and identify with the father. During this phase the boy makes the euphoric discovery of being not only separate from his mother, but different from her in a masculine way. He discovers Spider Man, Iron Man, Superman . . . and during this period, he reaches out to other males to be just like them.

But in homes in which the father is distant, detached, and critical, with mothers who are high-anxiety, intrusive and often discouraging of the boy's masculine strivings, there is a problem for the son who is temperamentally sensitive, gentle, and relational. Who will he identify with? On some level he knows he is a boy, but he is not quite sure that he wants to be one. His mother is the more attractive identification object; she is more sympathetic, closer to him; in some ways, more understanding of him, and she seems to "be more like him." In fact, if his mother is the narcissistic type, she may put him on a pedestal with a flattering idealization, and he may have trouble deciding where his mother stops and he begins.

And there is another problem: the boys he meets seem too rough; they feel like they are "not me"; and they often tease him for being sensitive. The girls, on the other hand, enjoy being his friend.

Many clients describe a negative experience with a father who was aloof, shaming, critical, and detached. If there was an older brother in the home, clients often described a fearful, hostile relationship with him. So this boy, due to his sense of gender incompleteness, struggles with an unspoken longing for male attention, affection and approval—a hidden, unsatisfied hunger, paired with a deep feeling of inferiority to other males.

And so we have the perfect storm—inborn temperamental sensitivity (*i.e.*, the "born that way" element), along with life experiences that do not facilitate the boy's gender-identity development; in fact, those experiences will have directly sabotaged it.

Those unmet gender needs then resurface in early adolescence in a sexualized form. Being ridiculed by his male peers, and feeling different from them, and sometimes experiencing sexual abuse by an older male who recognizes and then preys upon his insecurity and isolation, this boy longs to have a sense of masculine identity within him—but seeing no way to develop it, he now seeks to satisfy that need through eroticizing the boys that he has been secretly admiring.

Though he might try to "pray those feelings away," or deny them, they persist. He is then told by contemporary culture that if he has these feelings, that means he is gay, and to self-identify in any other way would be to deny his true nature.

What typically were the deciding factors that brought clients to the Thomas Aquinas Clinic? There are three main factors:

1. Sexual abuse—the client seeks treatment to resolve the trauma, because this experience has trapped him in a repetitive and self-defeating habit pattern—one which he has come to reject as being alien to his dignity as a man;

2. Many clients are persons of faith—Christian, Muslim, Jewish—religions whose sacred teachings instruct them that they were created to be heterosexual;

3. Simple dissatisfaction—some clients had tried gay relationships but found them shallow, compulsive, transient,

> unhealthy on both a physical and emotional level, and unfulfilling.

These clients, then, decided to search for a way out. They knew that there was more to their sexuality than what contemporary culture has been telling them. Searching online, they found Dr. Nicolosi, Sr.'s website, books, and videos. Many men found his compassionate, yet sometimes brash, direct, and politically incorrect discussion of homosexuality to be refreshingly frank, honest, and—most importantly—accurately reflective of their own backgrounds and lives.

This book contains many of the articles written over the years by Joseph Nicolosi, Sr.

A related form of this work is being done by his son, Joseph Nicolosi, Jr., who is also a psychologist.

To add memorial tributes to Dr. Nicolosi's life and work from friends and colleagues, visit his website at josephnicolosi.com and follow this link:

http://www.forevermissed.com/dr-joseph-nicolosi-sr/#about

## Introduction:

# How I Began this Work

*by Joseph Nicolosi, Sr., Ph.D.*

During my eight years of training toward a Ph.D. in clinical psychology, never was a word spoken about the causes or treatment of homosexuality. The entire topic from a clinical point of view was treated as nonexistent.

I think back to the year 1973, during my first year of internship, when I was a student in graduate school. During supervision time, another intern remarked that the American Psychiatric Association had just declassified homosexuality as a disorder. I turned to my supervisor and said: "But I thought it *was* a disorder."

With a shrug of the shoulders, he responded: "Of course it is."

"Then," I asked, "how did they decide to make it normal?" With the same shrug, he answered, "Politics."

Very soon after that 1973 decision, all psychological investigation of homosexuality as a disorder stopped; even within the psychoanalytic school of thought. Then, not long afterward, everyone was told that homosexuality was due to a gay gene and you were a hating homophobe if you dared question the gay-gene myth. If you had a homosexual client who was dissatisfied with his orientation, you were supposed to tell him, "Your gayness is who you are."

The lack of education on the subject made me poorly prepared to assist clients who came to me distressed by their homosexuality and unwilling to claim a gay identity. Still new to my profession and therefore reflexively loyal to its dictates, I simply listened, empathized and affirmed those clients in their distress.

In other words, I did nothing. But as I listened–which I was required to do, if nothing else—I noticed common themes in their boyhood: a strong and over-influential mother, to whom they were very close but whom they found frustrating; and a deep disappointment in relationship to a distant and seemingly uncaring father. Sometimes the fathers were cruel and abusive, but mostly they were just absent, busy and detached. If there was an older brother, he was feared and intimidating. And there were the usual horror stories of bullying at school.

Early on, I noticed an obvious difference in these clients' demeanor and self-presentation. As a group, they seemed self-conscious, passive and ill-at-ease. This was in contrast to my heterosexual clients who were in treatment for a variety of reasons; they more often appeared outspoken and self-assured. I later came to realize that these homosexual clients were displaying the "anticipatory shame posture," the expectation of being shamed by another man. They were demonstrating in their bodily posture the emotional detachment that lays the foundation for homosexual attraction.

As they spoke, I heard the common themes of an inferiority regarding their masculinity and a sexual attraction to men who possessed masculine traits that they themselves felt to be painfully lacking.

None of these family patterns were ever talked about among my colleagues, or mentioned in the literature. So with nothing available in the scientific literature of that time, I looked to the past. I began reading the old psychoanalytic papers, and there it was—all of those themes that my clients were speaking of. My first clue was in the work of Anna

Freud, who reported a successful treatment of three men based upon their awareness that they were attracted to men they envied. This discovery of envy was an essential clue.

For a while, then, I went back and forth, comparing what my clients told me with the writings of the early psychoanalysts. The old psychoanalytic literature was a lost intellectual tradition whose investigative approach contained the most penetrating understanding of homosexuality. Anna Freud again intrigued me when she described three men who diminished their homosexuality by understanding its reparative function.

As I went back and forth between my clinical observations and my psychoanalytic readings, I attempted to develop the most effective treatment for my clients. It became clear to me that homosexual behavior is an attempt at reparation for one's internal sense of gender deficit. Thus, the name of the treatment I developed: Reparative Therapy. Over time, I have come to understand that it is shame and not the homosexuality itself that should be the focus of Reparative Therapy. When we eliminate the shame, there is no homosexuality.

At the start of therapy, the clients typically convey an attitude of indifference toward the father, but with some investigation they soon expose a deep hurt and disappointment regarding their father's disinterest in them. In a lesser number of cases, there is explicit paternal verbal and physical abuse. Either way, their feelings for their fathers are distinctly negative. For their mothers, I found that beneath their close, even intimate relationships there is general irritation, and a deep resentment for her over-control. These are the same family patterns Sigmund Freud observed over 100 years ago, which were later confirmed by many other analysts; but no one talks about them today.

Later on I saw some homosexual clients who did not exactly fit this maternal profile, which led me to formulate a second type of homosexual—a type that I call the "post-gender-identity phase" homosexual.

As these men learned about themselves and experienced change, I felt a great satisfaction in achieving something that my profession was warning its members not to do. I had developed less respect for my profession—knowing, now, how vulnerable it was to the influence of politics, and seeing how its members were "sheep" who were following a scripted set of beliefs, not daring to think differently. I discovered that my clients were gaining greater understanding of their condition, and experiencing a reduction in their unwanted same-sex attraction. Not only was I doing what I was not supposed to do, but I was succeeding in it! More importantly, my clients were succeeding in fulfilling their hopes and dreams—a goal the psychological profession had told them they could not attain.

At the time of this writing (early 2017), with over 130 ongoing cases and six psychotherapists and interns, we at the Thomas Aquinas Psychological Clinic have the largest clinic in the world dedicated to the treatment of unwanted homosexuality. Few other psychotherapists dare to tackle this work.

The dominant political forces of our time have placed in disrepute an entire older intellectual tradition— the "golden years" of psychoanalytic thought, from the early 1920's to the late 60's. The 1950's, in particular, were an era of energetic debate among clinicians, theoreticians and students. The numerous panel discussions during this time allowed for free and open exchange about the phenomenon of same-sex attractions, which is impossible to imagine today in our politically correct climate.

Sadly, our new generation of psychotherapists is kept unaware of their chosen profession's buried treasures. They laugh at the old psychoanalytic truisms, seeing them as absurd metaphors, such as the saying (about homosexual men), "the bad breast is substituted by the good penis." But are they willing to investigate the meaning of these metaphors to gain the insight they offer?

One doctoral intern at our clinic, reading the transcript of a 1964 American Psychological Association Round Table Discussion (before politics had cut off debate), said in innocent irony: "It's amazing how accurately they understood the work we do today!"

Present-day defensiveness against any causative investigation is evidenced by the fact that there are more professional articles on the subject of "homophobia" today than on the investigation of homosexuality. The causation and treatment of homosexuality is just not addressed.

In an interview with cultural commentator Dennis Prager in 2014, Camille Paglia, a lesbian-feminist activist, said:

> Now you are not allowed to ask any questions about the childhood of gay people anymore. It's called 'homophobic.' The entire psychology establishment has shut itself down, politically . . . . So all the sophistication of analysis, in being able to analyze the family background [is] all gone.
>
> That entire discourse is gone. Everything is political now. It's really sick. It's a sick and stupid way of looking at human psychology. We are in a period now of psychological stupidity.

Indeed, since 1973, we have entered the Dark Ages of scientific investigation and intellectual exchange—what I call "The Great Shutdown." A dark and intimidating pall has been cast over the psychological profession, causing clinicians and researchers to avoid the topic and cede the discussion to colleagues who are themselves gay—a group which looks eagerly to the task as a chance to further their activism.

This intimidating environment of today has discouraged any research or professional dialogue. Nothing is written or communicated within the profession about causation or treatment. So, because nothing is happening today, we have to go back to the past.

Dismissed as personifications of an embarrassing era in the history of psychology, the early psychoanalytic writers could easily be forgotten. Scorned as bigots of an unenlightened past, they could be consigned—permanently—to the dustbin, if not for the new generation of dissatisfied homosexual clients seeking answers. This population of clients is not satisfied with the easy counsel of today, "Just work through your homophobia," and so they impel us as clinicians to offer ever-better answers.

The classic psychoanalytic literature has never been an easy read for anyone, especially today's mental-health professional who prefers simple "how-to" interventions rather than the work of pondering the functions of intra-psychic substructures. Part of the problem is due to the early psychoanalysts themselves. With their insular and "in-group" vocabulary, those psychoanalysts created a barrier to the outside world which protected their status as elite thinkers. I, too, have found myself puzzling over passages so dense and abstract that after several readings, they left me bewildered.

But that foundation, with its many case histories, still offers us much that is useful. Going back to the primary psychoanalytic sources written between 1886 and 2012, I have built Reparative Therapy upon their foundation—expanding, clarifying and revising those original observations through the insights I have gained during my own career.

May those insights be of good use to the hundreds of strugglers whom I have had the privilege to know.

Joseph Nicolosi, Sr.
Encino, California

## Chapter One:

# The Meaning of Same-Sex Attraction

*Our men seek to attain a state of authenticity, assertion, and attachment to other men. But homosexuality has brought them none of those things.*

During more than thirty years of clinical work with dissatisfied homosexually oriented men, I have come to see homosexual enactment as a form of "reparation." Through sex with other men, the person is attempting to "repair" attachment wounds that left him feeling deficient in male attention, affection and approval.

Homosexual sex temporarily relieves the three painful self-states that we repeatedly find in our same-sex attracted clients— most particularly, shame; difficulty with assertion; and the chronic depressive mood that I call the "Grey Zone."

Gay sex also helps a man break out of the constrictive social posture of the "good little boy," which has developed over the years into a False Self.

However, for my clients, homosexual enactment does not ultimately satisfy their deepest longings or fit their self-identity. It is a violation of their aspirations and a distortion of their life goals. Gay life is unsatisfying to them, so they enter therapy in the hope of reducing their unwanted attractions and developing their heterosexual potential.

Homosexual acting-out, for these men, is an attempt at restoring equilibrium in order to maintain the integrity of a fragile self-structure. Through erotic contact with another man, they unconsciously seek to attain a state of authenticity, assertion, autonomy, and gender-relatedness, but they have found that it eventually brings them none of those things—only a nagging feeling of inauthenticity, and still deeper discouragement.

## A Lifestyle of Hiding

Many same-sex attracted men live in a state of vigilance against the possibility of feeling shamed. This creates a lifestyle of hiding, avoidance, and passivity.

In clinical settings we have seen that anticipatory shame can become so intense as to approximate paranoia, with the frightening conviction that another person has the power to turn everybody against him. Past associations to this anticipation often go back to early adolescence, when a bully caused the other boys to reject him. Perhaps the shame originated even earlier, with the "omnipotent" (in the child's eyes) mother who, he feared, could cause family members to ostracize him.

Central to Reparative Therapy® is the task of helping the client transition out of the "shamed state" that creates the restricted posture of the False Self. We seek to move him into the assertive state that fosters the True Self.

Here are some guidelines, showing the qualities of self associated with each of the two states:

| TRUE SELF | FALSE SELF |
|---|---|
| Feels masculine | Feels unmasculine |
| Secure, confident, capable | Insecure, lacking confidence, incapable |
| Experiencing authentic emotions | Emotionally dead, or alternatively, hyperactive |
| Energized | Depleted |
| At home in body | Body is object, not self |
| Physical confidence | Anxious clumsiness |
| Feeling empowered, autonomous | Feeling controlled by others |
| Accepting of imperfection | Perfectionistic |
| Active, decisive | Passive |
| Trusting | Defensive posture |

| WITH OTHERS | |
|---|---|
| Attached | Detached |
| Outgoing | Withdrawn |
| Spontaneous | Over-controlled, inhibited, "frozen" |
| Forgiving, accepting | Retaliatory, resentful |
| Genuine, authentic | Role-playing, theatrical |
| Seeks out others | Avoidant |
| Humility | Self-dramatization |
| Aware of others | Constricted awareness |
| Assertive, expressive | Nonassertive, inhibited |
| Mature in relationships | Immature in relationships |
| Respectful of others' power | Resentful of others in power |
| Empowered | A victim |
| Integrated; open | Double life; secretive |

| | |
|---|---|
| Rapport with opposite gender | Misunderstanding of opposite gender |
| Sees other men as like self | Pulled by mystique of other men |
| NO HOMOSEXUALITY "Homosexuality rarely comes up for me. I can willfully visualize it - but it doesn't have that compelling quality." | HOMOSEXUALITY "I'm in that whole gay mindset. Sexual attraction to guys preoccupies and dominates my entire outlook." |

An important component of Reparative Therapy is teaching our clients to be conscious of what is happening to their minds and bodies when they are experiencing same-sex erotic attraction. When our clients attend to their bodies during such a moment, their first feeling is typically a sensation of tightness in the chest (fear) that is followed by a sinking, dropping sensation, with an internal collapse in the center of the body (shame); then, a genital arousal. This genital arousal is an attempt at reparation for the fear and shame evoked by the male image. (The compensatory nature of this erotic attraction is fundamentally different from heterosexuality.)

With homosexual men, sex is often used as a defense against a feared object. It is an attempt to incorporate, "take in," "master" and control something threatening outside of the self. It can function as a symbolic "acquisition," or a "possession" of the other person that is aggressive and not loving. One client described his sexualization of fear-provoking men as "the victory of the orgasm." Another, as "the orgasmic painkiller." As one client told me, "By giving him pleasure, I am in control. By controlling his pleasure, I control him."

Healthy sexuality, on the other hand, is characterized by love and mutuality, whereas a shame-based and fear-based use of sex is narcissistically motivated and ultimately empty and unsatisfying, leaving the client depressed.

## Neurobiological Considerations

Though a popular slogan today is "love is love," neurobiology in fact tells a different tale. Unlike heterosexual men, men with same-sex attractions were found, in one study, to show significant amygdala activity in their brains—a fear-driven response—when they are exposed to a homosexually arousing image. (Safron, *et al.*, 2007)

Although the amygdala is involved in numerous brain functions, it plays a major role in the processing of shame and fear. The authors of the Safron study believe that due to the speed of the neuro-imaging, the amygdala activation in gay men was not attributable to shame regarding social disapproval; social-referencing, they contend, would have taken longer to be generated. Another study reaches a similar conclusion: "[D]ifferent neural circuits are active during sexual arousal in homosexual and heterosexual men" (Hu *et al.*, 2008, p. 1890).

## Male Friendship vs. Erotic Attraction

Essential to the process of overcoming homosexuality is to encourage our clients to develop close friendships with heterosexual males. Through these intimate but non-erotic relationships they are able to internalize the three A's—attention, affection and approval—and in so doing, deepen their masculine identification. From our clinical work, we have found that true male friendship and homoeroticism will be mutually exclusive.

## Childhood Trauma and the Creation of the Shamed Self

Childhood trauma—which can take the forms of (often unintended) parental neglect, abuse, or simply parental physical absence—leaves the child with an emotional injury. This is particularly true if the child believes the trauma is his fault.

Shame is the introjection—the "taking into one's self"—of negative messages from an abusive, neglectful or malattuned parent. This dynamic was explained by Freud as a primitive defense against total loss of a "significant other." He said, "No child can risk the total rejection of the parent, who inevitably wields great power over his life—in fact, his very survival. To do so would require the intolerable conclusion, 'I am an orphan.'"

Psychic survival requires him to split from the self, and to join with the critical parent against the self. As Freud said: ". . . the result of which is that in spite of the conflict with the loved person, the love relationship need not be given up." (Freud 1917, p. 249)

So in order to maintain emotional connection, the child decides: "There is nothing wrong with mother (or father) but something bad in me (my maleness, my individuation from them) that deserves punishment."

As one client said, "Feeling like I'm 'no good' filled the void of being alone."

## Shame Messages for Masculinity

In various and subtle ways, the shamed son is led to feel that his growing and fragile sense of maleness—something he is, on one level, proud of—separates him from his father. A mother may perceive signs of a boy's growing masculinity as "vulgar" or somehow not "fitting" her "good little boy." Mothers of homosexuals often have poor relationships with the men in their lives—both fathers and husbands; thus, masculinity can be perceived by them as threatening, a perception which will be imposed upon her son.

A father may indirectly shame his son by ignoring the boy's attempts to emotionally attach. The internalized message that the fragile, sensitive son gets from paternal disregard is: "I'm not male enough to be accepted by this man . . . . He is right. There is something wrong with my male ambition for which I deserve to be punished." The son therefore renounces his hope for parental connection in the role of an independent male, but he still seeks love from that same person toward whom he feels hostility.

This contradictory hostile-dependency of the son toward the father is reenacted in adult sadistic-masochistic sexual behavior, where "part of me punishes another part of me." These two roles—as both the recipient of punishment, and the punisher—are acted out as mechanisms offering a sense of control and mastery over the past trauma. Through "identification with the aggressor," the masochist controls the inflictor of pain (the aggressor) and in so doing, he controls the extent and intensity of his own pain in the attempt to finally "conquer" the past trauma.

## Childhood Sexual Molestation: an Occasion for the Creation of the Shamed Self

Many gay men report sexual abuse by a male during their boyhood. By teaching the client to attend to his body during a homo-arousing moment, he discovers that the emergence of the shamed self is a precursor to his homosexual arousal. If his shame can be resolved, then the secondary effect—*i.e.* the drive toward homoeroticism—will diminish. In fact, the client learns that the greatest obstacle to the heterosexual outcome he desires is his anticipatory shame.

When the client links the past with the present, his perception of a homoerotic image gradually shifts from excitement to neutrality. This shift can lead the client either into the Assertive State or the Grief State. With the removal of the shame that was necessary for his same-sex arousal, the once-arousing image now instead, evokes a sense of loss. He begins to rediscover his authentic need for true male affection, quite separate from eroticism.

For this client, understanding this link between past trauma and present homosexual enactment is the first and necessary step toward self-compassion and the reduction of shame. Whatever the self-accusatory statement is, questioning the origins bring the client back to past events that created the erotic compulsion. The substitution of shame for self-compassion often leads to a more empathic view of other gay men for whom the client previously felt contempt.

Gay sex tends to represent a repetition compulsion, as evidenced in the client's relentless search to achieve "mastery" of the unavailable male, even though his efforts always prove self-defeating. As with all forms of repetition compulsion, this is a fantasy option—a futile grasping at self-completion.

On one level, this erotic drive represents a healthy, reparative drive to be proactive—an attempt to gain victory over a previous humiliating experience. But to the extent that it is a function of narcissistically-based illusions, it is doomed to defeat—because any attempt at resolving early attachment loss through erotic enactment will not work.

Through therapeutic Body Work* many men come to see that they have been attempting to gain male connectedness in a self-defeating way that protects them against feelings of deep grief. Beneath their homosexual behavior is the drive to gain authentic attachment. Through same-sex erotic contact, they are seeking resolution of the powerful and **normal** need to be known and loved by another man.

* *Body Work does not involve physical touch.*

## Chapter Two

# The Paradox of Self-Acceptance

This is the paradox of reparative therapy: *it is successful only if the client first faces and accepts himself, including his unwanted feelings.*

The more the person examines the thing inside himself that he rejects, and sees it in the light of truth, the more it dissipates. The task is not to look away from the feelings, but to look *through* them.

When we use the "Triangle of Containment" in therapy, the client is asked to focus directly on a homosexual thought or fantasy. At the same time, he should actively attend to his bodily sensations. While doing this, he is asked to stay connected to the therapist.

When the client is holding on to the homoerotic image, he will usually experience a simultaneous bodily arousal. (Some men describe it as a genital surge, a rush, or a "zap.") If he can accept his bodily homoerotic experience while staying connected to the therapist, the sexual feeling soon transforms into something else: the recognition of deeper, pain-generated emotional needs which have nothing to do with sexuality.

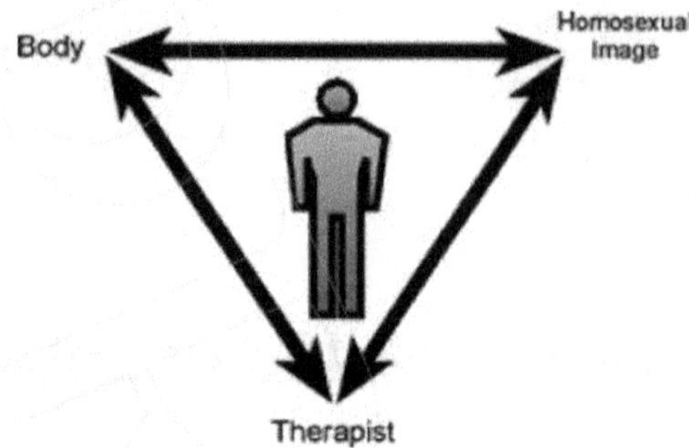


Re-experiencing the feelings openly in the presence of an accepting therapist helps remove that shame; the client is then better able to see his same-sex desire for what it is. One man described his liberation from shame by looking deeper into the homoerotic illusion. "Looking at it in the light of day," he said, "takes the 'leprosy' out of it."

When we push the shame aside—*facing the feared fantasies directly*—we see the true nature of the man's homoerotic attraction, which is about attachment loss.

When the man looks past that erotically charged male symbol—the icon of a missing part of his identity—he can begin to fulfill the same-sex attachment needs that are at the core of his deepest longings.

## Chapter Three

# Trauma as the Foundation of Homosexuality

In recent years, I've watched with dismay as the homosexual movement has convinced the world that "gay" requires a revised understanding of human nature.

The psychological profession is much to blame for this shift. Since up to the 1960s it was generally agreed that normality is "that which functions in accordance with its design," there was then no such thing as a "gay person," for humanity was recognized as naturally and fundamentally heterosexual. During my 30-plus years of clinical practice, I have seen the truth of that original understanding: emotionally and physically, we are designed for heterosexuality.

Homosexuality, rather than being part of our nature, is essentially a symptom of trauma. Some homosexual men may have been born with biological conditions (prenatal hormonal influences, inborn emotional sensitivity) that make them especially vulnerable to gender injury. But whether the primary influence on any particular person was biological or psychological, the result is the same: an interruption in the normal masculine identification process.

Homosexual behavior is a symptomatic attempt to "repair" the original wound that left the boy alienated from his innate masculinity.

This differentiates it from heterosexuality, which arises naturally from undisturbed gender-identity development.

Not all homosexuality takes the same path, but the conflict we see most often in homosexuality is this: the boy—usually a sensitive child, more prone than average to emotional injury—desires love and acceptance from the same-sex parent, yet feels frustration and rage against him because the parent is experienced by this particular son as unresponsive or abusive. (Note that this boy may have brothers who experienced the father differently.) The development of this son's homosexuality is, then, an erotic reenactment of his early love-hate relationship with the father.

Like all the "perversions"—and I use that term not to be unkind, but in the sense that homosexual development "perverts," or "turns a person away from," the biologically appropriate object of erotic attachment—same-sex eroticism contains an intrinsic dimension of hostility.

And so we see that homosexuality is inherently rooted in conflict: conflict about the acceptance of one's natural gender, conflict in the parent-child relationship, and usually, conflict regarding ostracism by same-sex peers. This means that dominance-submission and sadomasochistic themes will often contaminate gay relationships.

For the homosexually oriented man, sexuality is an attempt to incorporate, "take in," and "master" another male. It functions as a symbolic "possession" of the other person.

There are some exceptions to the trauma model of homosexual development. For example, we have found at our clinic another form of homosexuality that is characterized by a mutual, affectional attachment, most often seen in our adolescent clients and in some immature adults. In this type of homosexual attraction, there are no hostile-dependent features, but rather, a romantic adolescent quality—an infatuation that has a sexual manifestation. Such liaisons may be undertaken for a period of months or years and then be abandoned, never to be resumed, as this phase of attraction passes.

Other men successfully made the initial bond with their fathers, but the father was not effective enough to protect the boy from the trauma of a "crazy-making" mother; the boy then develops a longing for a salient man to intervene and "rescue" him, which becomes eroticized into homosexual attractions as he grows older.

Still, the general rule remains: If a child is traumatized in a particular way that affects gender, he will become homosexual, and if you do not traumatize a child in that particular way, the natural process of heterosexual development will unfold.

Another "trauma" model we have seen has its foundation in early sexual molestation. Many gay-identified men report sexual abuse by a same-sex person during their boyhood. This molestation is characterized as abuse, because it comes to the vulnerable (and usually lonely) child disguised as "love." Here is one client's account of an older teen who molested him:

> I wanted love and attention, and it got all mixed up with sex. It happened during a time when I really had no sexual interest in other boys . . . . I thought he [the abuser] was cool. He never gave me any attention unless he wanted to fool around. When we did get sexual, it felt special . . . . It felt exciting and intense, something between us, a shared secret. I had no other friends and my lousy relationship with my father didn't help. I was looking for friendship… [but] the intensity of the memory . . . I hate it. The whole thing is just disgusting, disturbing . . . . This is the root cause of my same-sex attraction.

This client had made the following association: "In order to receive the good, *i.e.* 'love' and 'attention,' I must accept myself as shameful and bad: engaging in activity which is 'frightening,' 'forbidden,' 'dirty,' and 'disgusting.'"

In therapy, as this client attended to the feelings in his body during an unwanted homo-arousing moment, he discovered that before he felt a homosexual feeling, he would invariably experience the sense of having been shamed by another man. In a reenactment of his childhood abuse, the "shamed self" proved to be a necessary prerequisite to his homosexual arousal.

The relationship between this client's past abuse and his present-day homosexual enactment is an example of a repetition compulsion. Repetition compulsion contains three elements: (1) attempt at self-mastery, (2) attempt at self-punishment, (3) avoidance of the underlying conflict.

In the search to find love and acceptance, the client with a repetition compulsion becomes entangled in repeating a self-defeating and self-punishing behavior, through which he unconsciously seeks to gain final victory and resolve his core injury.

For such men, the pursuit of fulfillment through same-sex eroticism is spurred by the fearful anticipation that their masculine self-assertion will inevitably fail and result in humiliation. They opt for a ritualized reenactment with the hope that, unlike all other past occasions, "This time, I will finally get what I want; with this man, I will find masculine power for myself," and "this time, the nagging sense of internal emptiness will finally disappear."

Instead, he has given one more person the power to reject him, shame him, and make him feel worthless. When the shame-producing scenario is played out over and over again, this only reinforces his conviction that he really is a hopeless victim and ultimately unworthy of love.

Gay men often report craving a sexual "adrenalin zap" which is heightened by the element of raw fear. There is an entire gay subculture of public sex that revels in the thrill of acting out in places like parks, public bathrooms and truck stops, and is erotically driven by excitement from the fear of discovery and exposure.

## Gay Sex as Intrinsically Dysfunctional

The act of sodomy itself is masochistic. Anal intercourse, as a violation of our bodily design, is unhealthy and anatomically destructive, damaging the rectum and spreading disease because the rectal tissues are fragile and porous. Psychologically, the act humiliates and demeans a man's dignity and masculinity.

Compulsive sexual acting-out, with its high drama and its promise of gratification, masks the deeper, healthier underlying drive to gain authentic attachment.

This dysfunction in the gay male world is undeniable. Scientific studies offer us evidence for the following sad comparisons:

—*Sexual Compulsivity* is more than six times greater among gay men.

—Gay men engage in *partner interpersonal violence* three times more often than do heterosexual men.

—Gay men engage in the *sadistic practices* at much higher rates than do heterosexual men.

—The incidence of *mood disorders* and *anxiety disorders* is almost three times greater among gay men.

—*Panic Disorder* is more than four times greater than for heterosexual men.

—*Bipolar Disorder* is more than five times greater than heterosexual men.

—*Conduct Disorder* is almost four times greater (3.8) than in heterosexual men.

—*Agoraphobia* (fear of being in public places) is more than six and a half times greater than among heterosexual men.

—*Obsessive-Compulsive Disorder* is more than seven times greater (7.18) than in heterosexual men.

—*Deliberate Self-Harm* (suicidality) is more than twice (2.58) to over ten times (10.23) greater than among heterosexual men.

—*Nicotine Dependence* is five times greater than among heterosexual men.

—*Alcohol Dependence* is close to three times greater than among heterosexual men.

—*Other Drug Dependence* is more than four times greater than that of heterosexual men.

Gay promiscuity is well illustrated in the classic research of McWhirter and Mattison, who reported in their book *The Male Couple* (1984), that of 165 relationships they studied, *not a single pair* of gay men was able to maintain fidelity for more than five years.

The authors—*a gay couple themselves*—were surprised to discover that outside affairs were not only *not* damaging to the relationship's endurance, but were in fact essential to its very survival. *In other words, gay men have to be unfaithful to each other if they want to stay together*. They conclude: "The single most important factor that keeps couples together past the ten-year mark is the lack of possessiveness they feel." (256)

By recognizing the love-hate dimension in homoerotic activity, we can empathize with the gay man's attempt at resolution of his childhood trauma through the endless search for another partner. This offers us a window of understanding as to why there continues to be a high level of psychiatric problems in the gay community in spite of unprecedented gains in the acceptance of homosexuality.

Homosexuality has no significance in the natural world other than as a "symptom"—a consequence—of unfortunate events. Otherwise it is otherworldly, a figment of fantasy and desire.

But through the help of social media, Hollywood and political force (which rapidly accelerated during the years of the Obama administration), a new definition of the human person has been invented. This linguistic sleight-of-hand has created a figment of the imagination. An erotic illusion has hijacked reality. Classical anthropology has been turned on its head, and a new man has been contrived. When a person labels himself "gay," he moves himself out of the natural realm and disqualifies himself from fully participating in human destiny.

From father to son to grandson to great-grandson, a man's seed is his link to the generations. Through his DNA, he lives on in other lives. When implanted into the woman's womb, his seed produces human life. But in homosexual sex, the seed of life is implanted in the rectum and associates itself with futility, decay and death.

In the natural sex act, however, the human race is preserved, and the man lives on through future generations. But in the trauma-driven sex act that violates our bodily design, his generative power is futile. And so the wisdom of the body presents this choice: choose *life,* or *decay and death.*

No wonder we see so much dissatisfaction in the gay world; because the man who lives in that world, on some level senses the futility of a gay identity. The attachments he forms will mean the termination of that long line of his ancestors who were once linked together, through the ages, in natural marriage.

In the real world, a gay identity makes no sense. Only as a symptom, as an eroticized reparation for attachment loss, does homosexuality have any meaning.

## Chapter Four

# Reparative Therapy®: a Pilgrim's Journey

*Something "old"—the False Self—must die in order for something new, and more beautiful, to be born.*

The men who come to us for help with unwanted sexual feelings are in the midst of a crisis that is disordering their lives. Their hearts and minds have been opened to the need to look deeply within.

Our "reparative" view of homosexuality offers a compassionate and non-blaming understanding of the development of homosexuality. But many gay-identified persons find the word offensive: "I don't need to be fixed, mended or repaired." Our answer is, "Of course not: no one can 'repair' another person!"

But in contrast to the gay-identified person who is offended by this term, our clients find comfort in our understanding of their homosexual behavior. We understand it as an unconscious attempt to "self-repair" their feelings of masculine isolation and inferiority. Their unwanted attractions are not just a negative force. These attractions represent their attempt to meet the normal, healthy needs that every man feels, *and should feel,* for male intimacy and connection.

Understanding this reparative concept increases our clients' self-acceptance and compassion regarding this desire for male intimacy, which previously evoked in them only confusion and shame.

The term "reparative," then, conveys an insight about the nature of homosexuality, which is that same-sex attraction is an unconscious effort at self-reparation. Through this shared perspective of the issue, client and therapist collaborate as they probe deeper for a fuller understanding of the client's experience.

Of course, the client's intent is to simply rid himself of what he sees as a "behavioral problem" as quickly as possible. However, there will be no quick fixes: to re-order the *dis*-order, he must first descend into the depths of his deeply felt emotions.

## Body Work

During therapy, the client will encounter a course of what we call Body Work. Body Work involves the development of self-attunement, and does not involve physical touching. It consists of three phases — (1) the first, defensive stage; (2) the core-affective encounter, and (3) a final, integrative phase.

Our client begins the session in the defensive phase, not wanting to face and fully feel the conflict in his life. His state of mind is dominated by self-protection as the therapist attempts to move him beyond his anxiety and into the Core-Affective phase, the place where he will encounter his deepest emotions.

Gradually surrendering his defenses, he will enter into and become overwhelmed by his deepest feelings about his personal struggle. This is the essence of Body Work; while maintaining emotional contact with the therapist, he must fully experience (on a body-memory as well as psychic level) his core-affective state, along with the tension responses in the body that hide, protect and retain those feelings.

## Cognitive Integration

Then we begin the Cognitive-Integration phase, where the client attempts to understand how his life history has influenced the behavioral decisions that have brought him into therapy. This is the period of meaning transformation, which integrates his life crisis into a larger perspective.

Those three phases of the psychological journey may be understood as a microcosm of the same personal transformation revealed in the epic themes of both classic Greek and religious literature. Across time and cultures, the three phases convey the same universal truth about human development.

The client believes his problem is merely one of unwanted attractions; but as he plumbs the depths of the unconscious, he discovers that his problem is really not so much about sexuality, as it is about everything else— particularly, it is a much deeper identity problem.

## The Universal Transformative Experience

In the epic poems of the Greeks, the transformative experience shows us a three-phase passage: exile, journey, and the return home. Christian literature portrays the three phases as descent, conversion, and ascent. Old Testament biblical stories depict sin, repentance, and grace. In the Book of Exodus, the great transition is the journey from slavery in Egypt to the Promised Land; in psychology, we see the state of slavery as the man's emotional repression, with the Promised Land being that of genuine self-knowledge, true wisdom, and self-autonomy.

This journey always begins with the warrior (or pilgrim) who must radically interrupt his everyday life to be confronted with a test. Our client, confronting his deepest emotions, like the warrior, will encounter frightening forces which are to be wrestled with and tamed.

## Returning Home: the Classic Tradition

In Ovid's *Metamorphoses* and Virgil's *Aeneid,* we have mythical tales of descent into the wilderness, and of progress through purification experiences—ending with a final, glorious ascent. Among the Greek mythologies, the allegory of the soul's progress is found in Homer's *Odyssey.* In the warrior Odysseus, we see a man cast on the ocean and tossed about in a small boat that brings home the lesson of the frailty of his human power.

## The Christian Tradition

To people of faith, this same quest to "journey home" is the struggle toward holiness. Within the Christian literary tradition we see the inspiration of the Biblical stories, foremost of which is Christ's crucifixion and death; his descent into Hell; and his final resurrection. In the New Testament (Luke 15:11-32), we see the parable of the prodigal son, who squandered his inheritance, then returned, chastened, and was ultimately redeemed. In the Hebrews' exodus from Egypt, we see a vivid description of Israel's escape from slavery, with the perilous desert crossing and fording of the Red Sea, and the ultimate arrival in the Promised Land. In John Bunyan's *The Pilgrim's Progress* and St. Bonaventure's *The Journey of the Mind into God,* the wayfarer takes a similar journey. In Dante's medieval poem, *The Divine Comedy,* we see the pilgrim traveling into the Inferno, through Purgatory, and then into Paradise. *The Divine Comedy* portrays the same three phases of interior transformation: descent, conversion, and finally, ascent.

## The Journey as Purification

In many of the texts about transformation, the journey is viewed as a process of purification. Successful completion of the process, in Greek mythology requires the purging of pride (hubris). In religious texts, the pilgrim must purify himself of the Seven Deadly Sins. Within both secular and religious traditions, this purging process is vividly experienced as necessitating a sort of "death."

Reparative Therapy acknowledges a similar process: we see the "death" of narcissistic and False-Self defenses with which the client on some level identifies, mistakenly thinking them to represent his True Self.

As we see it, something old (the False Self) must die in order for something new, and far more beautiful, to be born. This new birth requires the client's transformative discovery that life can be lived without those old defenses. When he surrenders the Shame Posture and begins to relate to others through the Assertive Self, he sees his True-Gendered manhood slowly emerge.

In Reparative Therapy, the client's journey ideally ends the same way: *with a return home to the woman*. In all these traditions, it is the feminine who is the giver of life. She is the mediator who puts into order the man's inner world.

It is this fulfillment of his masculine identity—which is the goal of Reparative Therapy—that permits the client to welcome this once-feared feminine power.

## Chapter Five

# Transgender Boys

> *"If I can **become** Mommy, then I take her into me, and never lose her . . . I must either **become** Mommy, or I cease to exist."*

I once appeared as a guest on the "Dr. Phil Show" in a television segment on children who think they are the opposite sex.

Another guest on the show was the mother of a transgendered boy; her son was living life as a girl. Several psychotherapists were also guests. They believed that transgenderism is normal and natural—and that parents should greet it with enthusiasm.

I took the opposite position; that children should not be encouraged to think of themselves—and live—as the opposite sex.

## "Imitative Attachment" in the Gender-Disturbed (GID) Boy

"Gender-Identity Disorder (GID) is primarily an attachment problem." This key concept, which I proclaimed during the Dr. Phil interview, was edited out. What stayed in the TV show, of course, were the words shouted at me by the angry, offended mother who wanted her boy to be accepted as a girl.

As a result, what could have been a fruitful discussion of psychodynamics was turned into little more than a yelling match. But this concept is, in fact, absolutely critical to an understanding of gender-disturbed children. None of the other therapists on the show discussed the underlying dynamics of the problem. They simply assumed, without evidence or inquiry, that the child was "born that way" and that the condition was normal and natural for that child.

GID children do not necessarily suffer from a lack of parental devotion. But to begin to understand the child, we must understand that in early infancy, the child's sense of self is very fragile, and is formed in relationship to the mother. The mother is the source and symbol of the child's very existence. It is a simple, biological reality that infants cannot survive without a nurturing figure.

Experts in the area of childhood gender-identity disorder (a diagnosis which has now been erased from the psychiatric manual) have found certain key patterns in the backgrounds of these children. A common scenario is an over-involved mother with an *intense, yet insecure, attachment* between mother and child. Mothers of GID children usually report having felt high levels of stress during the child's earliest years.

We often see severe maternal clinical depression during the critical attachment period (birth to age 3) when the gender-disturbed child is individuating as a separate person, and when his gender identity is being formed. The mother's behavior was often highly volatile during this time, which could have been due to a life crisis (such as a breakup in the marriage), or from a deeper psychological problem in the mother herself, such as borderline personality disorder, severe narcissism, or a hysterical personality type.

When the mother is alternately deeply involved in the boy's life, and then unexpectedly disengaged, the infant experiences an attachment loss—what we call "abandonment-annihilation trauma." The gender-disturbed children's response is an "imitative identification"—the unconscious idea that "If I *become* Mommy (*i.e.,* become female), then I take Mommy into me and I will never lose her."

This is the same dynamic that we see in the fetish, where the boy is "taking in a piece of Mommy" (her shoes, her scarf) and developing an intense (and later sexualized) attachment to an object that is associated with the person (the mother) who provides his primal sense of security.

The infantile dynamic of "imitative attachment" is such that "keeping Mommy inside" becomes truly a life-or-death issue—"Either I become Mommy, or I cease to exist." This explains why gender-disturbed boys are willing to tolerate social rejection for their opposite-sex role-playing—*it feels like death* to abandon this perception of themselves as a girl.

The phenomenon of "imitative attachment" explains why gender-disturbed boys do not display femininity in a natural, biologically based way, as do girls; but rather, they demonstrate a one-dimensional, clinging caricature of femininity—exaggerated interest in girls' clothes, makeup, purse-collecting, *etc.* and mimicry of a feminine manner of speaking.

As one mother explained to me, "My GID boy is more 'feminine' than his sisters."

## "Born that Way?"

Although I believe gender disturbances always involve some kind of attachment problem, there may also be biological influences that lead some children in that direction.

One psychiatrist on the Dr. Phil show discussed a recent, credible biological theory. For at least some boys who want to be girls, there may have been an unusual biological developmental problem, during the time when the then-unborn child was being formed in the uterus. The theory is that this may have resulted in the incomplete masculinization of the boy's brain. These boys' brains are more feminine than other boys'; in extreme cases, they may grow up feeling like girls trapped in a male body.

This biological theory has some credible support—in fact, it may well explain a few cases of gender disturbance as a biological developmental *error*. But science has, as yet, no test that can confirm that this brain event has actually occurred.

However, we do know that *human emotional attachment* changes the structure of the infant's brain *after birth*. So if we encourage the gender-disturbed boy to act like a girl, we will never know to what extent he *could have* become more comfortable with his normal biological sex if his parents had been committed to actively reinforcing his appropriate gender identity and working to address the psychological problem of imitative attachment with the mother.

In our clinical work with GID boys, we see genuine, positive changes occur. We never shame the child for acting like a girl; we reinforce him for biologically appropriate behaviors and encourage him to grow more comfortable as a boy, thus helping him to sense that being a boy (and internalizing a masculine identity) is safe, and that being a boy is good.

No one on the Dr. Phil Show mentioned the dire implications of taking the opposite approach—actively preparing a boy for future sex-change surgery by giving him puberty-blocking hormones. *Surgery can never truly change a person's sex.* Doctors can remove the male genitals and form an imitation of the female sex organs, but they cannot make the simulated organs functional. The DNA in a boy's cells *throughout his body* cannot be changed with surgery; he will always be a boy. Thus, after sex reassignment surgery, he will still carry a male genotype.

We believe that every effort should be made to help a gender-disturbed boy accept his biological maleness, and be comfortable in life with the intact (not surgically mutilated) body with which he was born. To go along with the boy's fantasy that he can be a girl is in fact, child abuse. Even after genital mutilation surgery and hormone treatment, every cell of his body will continue to proclaim the truth that he is, in fact, a male.

## Chapter Six

# Mother – Son Boundary Violations as Blocks to Heterosexual Feelings

*To the male, the feminine must always be mysterious and "other than me."*

When the male homosexual client is exploring his ability to feel attracted to women, we sometimes encounter a sudden block. This often traces back to the boy's early experience with an intrusive and over-intimate mother. The following are some examples.

A client and I were doing Body Work on an attractive female image. As he gazed at the photo, he felt himself slowly developing warm, close feelings. But just as he was beginning to enjoy the pleasant sensations in his body, he hit a sudden barrier. He felt a rigidity in his chest (*i.e.*, fear). When we analyzed the problem, a jolting memory came up of his mother "playfully treating me like a baby" by taking her breast out and putting it to his mouth. He was ten years old—a preteen at the time—and the incident, which was supposed to be a joke, had brought up alarming, incestuous feelings which he had felt an anxious need to suppress. In fact, he had "forgotten" those feelings until this moment.

Another mother, a midwife in a small town, was called to help with a birth, and she took her seven-year-old son (who later became my adult client) along with her. The mother allowed her son to watch the delivery, and to this day, my client recalls the vivid image of the pregnant woman's bloody vaginal area and of her terrified screaming. This early, and (to him) horrifying experience of a woman's reproductive organs created an association that he was unable to erase. From that time forward, he felt a sense of revulsion whenever he thought of intimately touching the female body.

Another client told me of an incident when he was about thirteen. He was talking to his mother about his anxieties regarding having a girlfriend, and his inexperience about what to do or say. The mother suggested that the two of them—mother and son—practice kissing together. This client did not need to read Sigmund Freud to see the connection between that incident and his later feelings of apprehension toward women. His mother's total disregard for normal mother-son boundaries formed a barrier which prevented the client from developing heterosexual attraction. By default, he turned to the "safety" of homosexuality.

Many clients tell me that they and their mothers showered together. The mothers thought such an experience would make their sons feel relaxed about the human body, but instead, they produced the opposite effect in their sons—alarm about the appearance of incestuous feelings.

Other clients remember disturbing memories of their mothers walking around the house naked, an image which left them with defensive feelings of disgust. Some mothers also insisted on frequent cuddling and hugging, even as their sons got older.

In such situations, the feminine body becomes not a mysterious attraction, as it does for heterosexual men, but rather it becomes an object of dread. For the man who develops homosexually, the male body, in contrast, has no negative childhood associations of boundary violations and therefore, it represents a "safe haven" from the intrusive feminine.

Mothers who are flirtatious with their sons in an erotic manner are seeking to meet their own needs, to the neglect of their sons'. Their motivations could range from mere careless naiveté, to desire for narcissistic gratification, especially when the son becomes a substitute for a husband who has been disappointing to her. Thus the mother turns the son into a sort of plaything and fails to acknowledge his masculine dignity.

Mothers must always be sensitive to the healthy physical and emotional boundaries that are required by the young boy to develop heterosexually. To the male, the feminine must always be mysterious and "other than me," rather than intrusive, controlling, over-familiar, and suggestive of the threat of incestuous attraction, as so many of our homosexual clients report from their childhoods.

## Chapter Seven

# Working with Teenagers

*The reparative therapist does not simply accept, at surface level, the client's sexual and romantic feelings.*

Why is Reparative Therapy for teenagers so controversial? Opponents of the practice say that it involves shaming the client, causing him to deny his true self, and breaking up family ties. Treatment for minors (and in some states in the U.S., for adults) has now been outlawed in response to pressure from gay activists.

One such gay activist, Sam Brinton, has testified (while crying) to legislators that his two-year-long therapy as a minor involved "torture," "shaming," and "shock treatments," but says he just "can't remember" the offending therapist's name. First he claimed the therapist was a religious counselor, but when the legislative effort got underway to outlaw therapy by professionals, he changed his testimony to say his therapist was a licensed professional.

A video is available on YouTube that exposes Brinton's inconsistencies—and his personal life as a cross-dresser and sadomasochist who imitates acts of bestiality for recreation—but Brinton continues to provide this testimony to credulous legislators, sobbing while he urges them to ban reparative therapies so no other person will be "tortured" as he was. As of this writing, his testimony has never been challenged on the public record.

## The Client Sets the Goals

Yet, as with all good therapy, Reparative Therapy® never involves coercion. The client seeks assistance to reduce something distressing to him, and the therapist agrees to share his professional experience to help him. The two enter into a collaborative relationship, agreeing to work together to reduce the client's unwanted attractions and explore the possibility of his heterosexual potential.

The foundation of Reparative Therapy, as with all legitimate therapy, is the establishment of this therapeutic alliance. This is defined as follows: client and therapist agree to work together toward clearly defined objectives, *as defined by the client.* The client is encouraged to explain what his goals are for each session, *i.e.,* to bring into each session his "identified conflict." The client must always lead.

This collaborative relationship must not, of course, include imposing techniques which attempt to "cause" sexuality change.

The therapy utilizes four basic methods of intervention. All four methods will tend to reduce, or perhaps even eliminate, sexual or romantic attractions toward individuals of the same sex. But no outcome can be guaranteed, and therapy is difficult.

There must be an understanding from the outset that success will be achievable along a continuum from complete change, to partial change (the most common outcome being management and reduction of the unwanted feelings), to, for some people, no change at all.

Some clients will give up the struggle and decide to return to a gay lifestyle. Others, particularly religious clients, will ultimately decide to accept the persistence of their unwanted feelings and make a commitment to chastity, using the tools they have learned to keep their unwanted feelings in the background.

Sometimes, the client does not know what he wants, as is often the case with the teenager whose parents urge him to come into treatment.

In those cases, if the teenager does decide to come in, we agree NOT to work on his homosexuality, and the therapeutic alliance is founded upon some other of the client's goals, such as managing parental disapproval without family breakup, or dealing with problems of peer rejection.

## Most Therapists Fail to Ask Questions

The reparative therapist does not simply accept at a surface level the client's sexual or romantic feelings and behaviors, but rather invites him into a non-judgmental inquiry into his deeper motivations. The therapist must always ask "why" and invite the client to do the same.

The gay-affirmative therapist (*i.e.*, today's typical clinician), approaches the subject differently. Trained to affirm homosexuality without any inquiry, he addresses the homosexual attractions "phenomenologically" (*i.e.* accepting them at face value as a simple phenomenon without questioning their origins). This is a highly unprofessional omission.

The reparative therapist, in contrast, goes much deeper: he recognizes, for example, that a teen may believe he is gay for a variety of reasons that have nothing to do with his core sexual orientation.

A teenager's sexual feelings may be rooted in a need for acceptance, approval, or affection from males, or may reflect his loneliness, boredom, or simple curiosity. He may engage in same-sex behavior for adventure, money, peer pressure; or to express hostility in a sadomasochistic manner against male peers, or just to express simple rebellion. Sometimes he finds the challenge of dating a girl too daunting, whereas sex with males is found easily. He may also find himself reenacting an early trauma of sexual molestation by another male.

A higher-than-average percentage of homosexually oriented men were sexually abused in childhood by an older male. One study found that 46 % of homosexual men compared with just 7 percent of heterosexual males reported homosexual molestation. The same study also found that 22% of lesbians reported homosexual molestation compared with just 1% of heterosexual women. (Tomeo, *et al.*, 2001) In those cases where the person was molested in childhood, homosexual behavior reenacted in adulthood can represent a repetition compulsion more than an orientation.

Indeed, a teenager may become convinced that he is fundamentally homosexual through the influence of a persuasive adult—a gay-affirmative therapist, mentor, teacher, or even his own molester. Such influential adults could succeed in swaying an uncertain youth that homosexuality is, for him, simply inevitable.

Homosexual behavior may also reflect some kind of developmental crisis that has evoked insecurities, prompting the fantasy that he can receive protection from a stronger male. Additionally, insecurities regarding the opposite sex (hetero-phobia) may also prompt the search for the perceived safety and ease of finding a partner for same-sex behavior.

Environmental factors (incarceration, or living in a residential treatment facility) may promote homosexual behavior and consequent gay self-labeling. In addition, gay self-identification may represent a political or ideological statement of rebellion against the larger culture, as seen in radical-feminist lesbianism in the women's movement.

These and many other examples of homosexuality often appear in adolescence but then discontinue as the teen moves on to adulthood. This is confirmed by studies which show that as these teens get older they are increasingly less likely to self-identify as gay.

A 1992 study of 34,707 Minnesota youth reported that 25.9 % of 12-years-olds were uncertain if they were heterosexual or homosexual.[1] In contrast, only about 2 to 3 percent of adults eventually label themselves as homosexual. This means that almost 24% of these "sexually questioning" teens could erroneously be identified as homosexual if they are affirmed as gay by a gay-affirmative therapist, school counselor or an on-campus gay club.

For all these reasons the teenager deserves the right to explore the reasons he thinks, feels, acts or believes he is gay.

## Letting a Child Decide

I once received a call from a psychologist who had heard that I specialized in the treatment of homosexuality. His client was a 13-year-old boy who thought he might be gay, and he wanted some advice. I answered the psychologist's questions, giving him some direction about his understanding of the case. After about twenty minutes, I said to him, "But tell me—I'm not clear about your approach. Are you trying to encourage his heterosexual potential, or are you affirming his gay identity?"

The psychologist answered, "I'm letting the boy decide."

Of course, as psychotherapists we must not coerce or "over-persuade" in therapy. Life decisions must ultimately be those of the client, and we must be clear that we can accept our clients' choices—whatever they may be. Clients must be aware that gay-affirming therapy is available, even if we ourselves don't provide it. But along with those obligations, there are other ethical questions. How can we encourage a *13-year-old boy* to make the enormously significant decision to claim an alternative sexual identity?

## Not a Decision to be Made by a Teenager

Many school counselors direct confused teenagers to gay community centers to see if being gay "feels comfortable" for them. The gay community embraces these unhappy and searching youngsters. Many of them discover an exciting sense of belonging—as well as early initiation into promiscuous sex—in a welcoming community when they are barely into puberty.

According to the reports of school counselors, even heterosexual teenagers—encouraged by some AIDS Awareness Programs to find out if they enjoy sexual pleasure with males—are now beginning to proclaim themselves "bisexual."

Clearly, there is a period of sexual-identity confusion when a young person can be easily influenced in either direction.

The early teen years are a *critical period*. Should a youngster be encouraged to try gay sex? As psychiatrist Jeffrey Satinover says:

> The experience of pleasure creates powerful, behavior-shaping incentives. For this reason, when biological impulses—especially the sexual ones—are not at least partially resisted, trained and brought under the civilizing influence of culture and will, the pressure to seek their immediate fulfillment becomes deeply embedded in the neural network of the brain . . .
>
> What starts out relatively free, becomes less so . . . .[2]

What about the teen's parents? Do they approve of their son being introduced into a notoriously promiscuous community? What about the life-threatening health risks?

All things considered, the teen years are a good time to consider the question, "Who am I?" and "What do I value?" However, they are a poor time to engage in sexual-identity decisions that will have life-changing emotional consequences—as well as *life-threatening* physical risks.

## Endnotes

[1] Remafedi, G., Resnick, M., Blum, R., and Harris, L., "Demography of Sexual Orientation in Adolescents," *Pediatrics* 89 (1992)., pp. 714-21.

[2] Satinover, J., *Homosexuality and the Politics of Truth,* Grand Rapids, MI: Baker Books (1996).

## Endnotes

## Chapter Eight

# The Four Principles of Reparative Therapy®

*The gay-affirmative therapist and the reparative therapist are different: one seeks to affirm and deepen the client in a gay identity; the other, to guide the client as he searches for an underlying, heterosexual core.*

The four principles of Reparative Therapy are, first, the therapist's disclosing of his own views; second, his encouragement of value-free inquiry; third, to help the client to resolve past trauma; and fourth, to educate the client regarding the associated features of homosexuality.

## (1) Disclosing Versus Imposing

From the very start of therapy, the therapist should disclose his views on homosexuality; not only those he holds as a scientist-practitioner, but also his views from a personal, philosophical and worldview perspective. Similarly, the gay-affirmative therapist should disclose his philosophical views to the client; however, he or she generally does so from a quite different perspective—one that sees homosexuality as a normal and healthy developmental path that is equivalent to heterosexuality.

The client needs to be clear about the reparative therapist's different understanding of homosexuality: the reparative therapist sees this condition as an adaptation to childhood trauma.

At the same time, the client must have space to explore his own sexual identity and make his own self-determination. No therapist should pressure or manipulate him to adopt the same viewpoint as the therapist does. Indeed, he must accept and value the client as a person, no matter what his sexual orientation, behavior or self-label.

## (2) Encouraging Inquiry

While the client may be motivated to enter therapy to reduce his same-sex attraction (SSA), *the reparative therapist does not suggest any techniques that attempt to eliminate these feelings. Such attempts never work.* Rather, he invites and encourages the client to go deeper—to inquire. The client is thus encouraged to ask questions of himself, and to look into the feelings, wants and desires that lie beneath his SSA.

This brings us to another important rule of Reparative Therapy: The therapeutic alliance must include the mutual understanding that the client must always feel free to disagree with the therapist.

## (3) Resolving Past Trauma

Reparative Therapy views most same-sex attraction as reparation for childhood trauma. Such trauma may have been explicit, such as sexual or emotional abuse, or implicit in the form of negative parental messages regarding the child's selfhood and gender. Exploring, isolating and resolving these childhood emo- tional wounds often results in reducing unwanted same-sex attractions.

## (4) Education

It is the responsibility of the therapist not to withhold information that can be of use to the client. What the client does with that input is left for him to decide.

The reparative therapist is better informed than most general-practice mental-health professionals about same-sex attraction. His educational responsibility consists of three general areas:

**(a) Causation.** Research shows that same-sex attraction is associated with particular types of negative peer and family experiences. (Bieber *et al*, 1962; Green, 1996) When combined with a sensitive nature in the client, the consequent trauma tends to have damaging effects on the development of the male child's individuation from the mother, as well as on gender identity. The focus of treatment is identifying and resolving those traumatic ex-periences. (Bieber,et.al.,1962; Greenson, 1968; Tabin,1985; Nicolosi, Byrd and Potts, 2002)

**(b) Underlying Motivations.** There is a substantial body of evidence supporting the understanding of at least some forms of homosexual orientation as based upon disturbances in gender-identity formation. (Coates, 1990; Green, 1993; Horner, 1992; Fast, 1984; Coates and Zucker, 1988; Nicolosi, Byrd and Potts 2002) The fulfillment of those needs in adulthood can reduce, and sometimes eliminate, same-sex attraction. (Nicolosi, Byrd, and Potts, 2002)

**(c) Health Consequences.** As part of his discernment process, the client deserves to know the long-term medical and emotional liabilities associated with a gay lifestyle, including the common maladaptive behavioral patterns.[2] The timing and manner of delivery of these educational opportunities should be determined by the therapist's sensitivity to the client.

All such therapeutic interactions are in accord with the NARTH (National Association of Research and Therapy for Homosexuality) *Practice Guidelines for Treatment of Unwanted Same-Sex Attractions and Behaviors*. These guidelines ensure respect for the client and offer ethical parameters for treatment and educational interventions.

Reparative Therapy fully complies with California law, which directs the therapist to (A) "provide acceptance, support, and understanding of clients or the facilitation of clients' coping, social support, and identity exploration and development, including sexual orientation-neutral interventions to prevent or address unlawful conduct or unsafe sexual practices; and (B) [to] not seek to change sexual orientation." [3]

However, subsequent to that initial exploration, the gay-affirmative therapist and the reparative therapist will eventually part ways—the former to affirm and deepen the client in a gay identity; the latter to guide the client as he searches for what he believes to be an underlying heterosexual core.

---

## Endnotes

[1] "All the Facts about Youth and Homosexuality," NARTH, The National Association for Research and Therapy of Homosexuality (www.narth.com).

[2] *Journal of Human Sexuality* 1 (2009); *see also* Winn, R. (2012), *The Gay and Lesbian Medical Association*, "Ten Things Gay Men Should Discuss with Health Care Providers," wwwglma.org.

[3] Cal. Bus. & Prof. Code, Div. 2 (Healing Arts) Art. 15 section 865 (A)(2). As written by Dr. Nicolosi, who passed away in 2017, this paragraph was originally based on Senate Bill 1172, which was subsequently approved and became law on January 1, 2019.

## Bibliography

Bieber, I., Dain, H., Dince, P., Drellich, M., Grand, H., Gundlach, R., Kremer, M., Rifkin, A., Wilbur, C., and Bieber T. (1962), *Homosexuality: A Study of Male Homosexuals.* New York: Basic Books.

Greenson, R. (1968), "Disidentifying from mother: its special importance for the boy." In *Explorations in Psychoanalysis*, pp. 305-12. New York: International Universities Press.

Coates, S. (1990), "Ontogenesis of boyhood gender identity disorder." *Journal of the American Academy of Psychoanalysis* 18:414-418.

Coates, S. and Zucker, K. (1988), "Gender Identity Disorder in Childhood." In *Clinical Assessment of Children: A Biopsychosocial Approach*, Eds. C.J. Kestenbaum and D.T. Williams. New York: New York University Press.

Fast, Irene (1984), *Gender Identity, A Differentiation Model; Advances in Psychoanalysis Theory, Research, and Practice,* vol. 2, University of Michigan: The Analytic Press.

Green, Richard (1993). *The "Sissy Boy Syndrome."* New York: Harper Collins.

Horner, Althea (1992), "The role of the female therapist in the affirmation of gender in the male patient," *Journal of the American Academy of Psychoanalysis* 20, n. 4, pp. 599-610.

Nicolosi, Joseph (1991, 2020), *Reparative Therapy of Male Homosexuality: a New Clinical Approach,* Northvale, N.J.: Jason Aronson; Tarzana: Liberal Mind Publishers.

Nicolosi, Joseph (1993, 2021), *Case Stories of Reparative Therapy.* Northvale: Jason Aronson; Tarzana: Liberal Mind Publishers.

Nicolosi, Joseph (1993), "Treatment of the non-gay homosexual man," *Journal of Pastoral Counseling,* vol. 28, pp. 76-82.

Nicolosi, Joseph (2009), *Shame and Attachment Loss, The Practical Work of Reparative Therapy,* Downers Grove: InterVarsity Press, pp. 23-6.

Nicolosi, J., Byrd, A.D., Potts, R.W. (2002). "A meta-analytic review of treatment of homosexuality," *Psychological Reports* 90, pp. 1139-52.

Nicolosi, J., and Nicolosi, L.A. (2002), *A Parent's Guide to Preventing Homosexuality,* Downers Grove: InterVarsity Press.

Remafedi, G., Resnick, M., Blum, R. and Harris, L. (1992) "Demography of Sexual Orientation in Adolescents," *Pediatrics* 89, pp.714-21.

Rekers, George (1995), "Homosexuality: Developmental risks, parental values and cntroversies," in *Handbook of Child and Adolescent Sexual Problems*, G. Rekers, Ed., N.Y.: Lexington Books.

Satinover, J.B. (2007), "The 'Trojan Couch': how the mental health associations misrepresent science," National Association for Research and Therapy of Homosexuality (NARTH), https://www.semanticscholar.org/paper/The-%22-Trojan-Couch-%22-%3A-How-the-Mental-Health-Satinover/ 8ba2e0abf9e8d921bbb2447eab90f8b47c52ab1b

Tabin, Johanna (1985) *On the Way to the Self: Ego and Early Oedipal Development,* New York: Columbia University Press.

Tomeo, M.E., Templer, D.I., Anderson, S. (2001), "Compaative data of childhood and adolescence molestation in heterosexual and homosexual persons," *Archives of Sexual Behavior* 30, No.5.

Zucker, K., and Bradley, S. (1995). *Gender Identity Disorder and Psychosexual Problems in Children and Adolescents,* New York: Guilford.

Zucker, K. and Green, R. (1996), "Psychosexual disorders in childhood and adolescence," *J. of Child Psychiatry* 33, 107-51.

Chapter Nine

# The Damage Inflicted by a Narcissistic Parent

> *Children of narcissistic parents don't know who they are. The parents' love is conditional; they "love" the child according to how that child makes them feel.*
>
> *So, to protect his individual integrity, the child may assert himself as "other than" the parent and the gender he represents.*
>
> *This often results in homosexuality and transgenderism.*
>
> *The following is a description of the narcissistic personality and the effect narcissists have on the people who are in relationship with them.*

Narcissistic people may be well-intended, even benevolent. Yet they create havoc in the lives of the people around them.

Your first encounter with such a person may leave you charmed. You feel important, the center of the narcissist's attention. Yet you will also come away feeling strangely dissatisfied and irritated. You will have a vague perception of having been taken advantage of, and "used"—yet you can't quite put your finger on what caused that feeling.

All of us possess some degree of narcissistic features. But we are speaking here about the person for whom narcissism is the primary, organizing character trait.

## Children of Narcissists

The narcissistic parent believes he "loves" the child, and indeed he may do so in his own limited way; yet he steals the child's uniqueness. The child becomes, for the parent, an object for gratification. When the child expresses something unique about himself, if it doesn't gratify the image the parent has for the child, the parent will either react negatively, or not react at all. This message is conveyed non-verbally, and goes "under the radar" of conscious awareness.

The messages from the parent are conveyed in four ways—facial expression, vocal tone, body language and context. For an example of context, a boy comes home from school, and happily announces to his mother that he got an "A" on an exam, and the mother says, "Are you hungry?" The boy mutters no, and quietly goes to his room. Somehow he feels deflated, but can't put his finger on why. The mother's asking "Are you hungry?" unconsciously communicates the unimportance, for her, of his achieving something that he (but not she) values. To the sensitive child, her reaction conveys devaluation, diminishment, and for him, becomes a shame moment.

Narcissistic people are often charming, and within five minutes of meeting such a person, you may have the feeling that you have known them all your life—there is an instant sense of familiarity; they make you feel good about yourself. But you are walking into a trap. One could say "they flatter your pride before they strike"; but "pride goeth before a fall."

As an example of the "deflation" that narcissists cause, a young couple came to me who had had been trying to adopt a child from overseas; finally, they were approved for the adoption of the child they had been waiting for. The couple could not wait to have lunch with her mother to announce the good news, and she eagerly accepted their invitation. When the woman told her mother that a child would finally be coming home with them, the mother clapped her hands joyfully and cried, “I knew it, I knew it . . . I had a feeling, just the other day I had a dream. I can’t believe it, I think I’m psychic!” The young couple looked at each other across their chicken salads, feeling strangely deflated. This special event had somehow become, not about the new baby, but about Mum—and her having the gift of being psychic.

I think of many people I have known with narcissistic parenting styles. There’s the mother with a “need” to keep her son dependent; she still has him in diapers at five years old. There is the obese mother who puts coke in her toddler’s baby bottle because of her unconscious “need” to have the girl grow up overweight just like her. And there’s the father who discourages his physically awkward son from going to the gym because he doesn’t want a male rival in the family.

A number of years ago, I remember reading a news story (uncritically reported by the press) about a lesbian couple who were deaf; they sought out a sperm donor with congenital deafness so their child would stay locked into their own silent world.

## The New Mantra of Psychologists: “Who Am I to Say?”

Why does my profession have so little to say about human motivations? Past psychoanalytic history is rich with case histories that provided so much insight into our unconscious lives. Today, family influences are downplayed among psychologists—partly so as not to “blame” parents and cause pain, and partly to play into the popular misconception that we are the primary architects and designers of our own selves. As a result, my profession’s study of human life has become superficial, empty, and unsatisfying. Today’s psychologist makes very little inquiry under the surface when a client desires to self-identify as gay or transgender. The desire “just is,” according to this attitude, and is taken by the psychologist at face value. This is a tragic situation.

In fact, the many brilliant insights of the classic psychoanalysts have been buried and forgotten, much to the detriment of my (increasingly irrelevant) profession.

To return to the nature of narcissism; it is a handicap which limits a person's full participation in the emotional give-and-take of life. There is a "vampire" quality of sucking the dignity out of the other person. Even when the narcissist does give, his giving will be limited; before very long, he will bring the focus back to himself and how the other person's actions make him feel. This overshadows the narcissist's ability to experience true, lasting empathy for the other.

Yet accurate empathy is essential to our very humanity. Our ability to feel the other person's feelings, to attune ourselves to another's pains and passions, demonstrates the essence of our humanity. Thus the narcissist is deprived of the community of life. Usually, he is blind to his deep character flaw—"I am so generous, I give them everything; why doesn't my family want to spend time with me?"

The narcissist does not, in fact, feel very good about himself; his spontaneous, authentic self was likely not affirmed by his own (also narcissistic) parent.  His gestures and words are geared toward image, and therefore are studied; the improvisational nature of normal human give-and-take is instead, stylized. How he appears to others is a subject that can never be far from his mind.

When narcissists reach old age, losing their attractiveness and their sources of pride and power, they are angry, depressed and bitter. They are left alone by family members and wonder why. They spend their final days mulling over a litany of resentments toward loved ones who, in order to protect themselves, have learned to avoid them. They are trapped in the living hell of self-reference which, for a time—when things were going their way—was gratifying, but which in old age, comes to feel like they are wandering around in a disorienting hall of mirrors.

## The "Withholding / Introverted" Type of Narcissist

"John" is a highly intelligent engineer, but not a particularly emotional man. He has been very successful in his field but is not popular with his colleagues. He does not have the charming personality of the giving/extroverted type of narcissist. But John is very high-functioning; his home and business are well-run and he is known as reliable and competent. Conversation with him is, however, vaguely annoying; if a colleague mentions something new he has done, or a place to which he has just travelled, John remains quiet until he has an opportunity to tell the speaker a story of his own that it makes him feel good to relate. (Hearing of someone else's good fortune is vaguely annoying to him.)

A young undergrad at a social gathering of student engineers enthusiastically told John that he had just been to Tahiti. Rather than affirming the student's enthusiasm about his travel experience, John's sole response to him was, "Now, *that's* the one country *I* haven't been to yet!"

When he visits his grandkids, John always wants to be sure the visit was worth it to him, and he "has fun." He won't babysit when his daughter and son-in-law actually need him; he waits until loneliness strikes and he feels the need to see the kids. When he does babysit and the kids don't fuss or cry, he reports that it "felt good."

When a new grandchild comes, the first news he relates is something self-referential—"I've got a red-haired granddaughter!" or, "I've got a second grandson!" instead of conveying news about the health of mother and baby. He describes the child in terms of the features that look like his own— "The boy has my feet." "He has my eyes." If someone points out that the child has his daughter-in-law's nose, John's silence indicates disinterest. At family gatherings, he is sure to be the first one to reach the buffet table to fill his plate.

Those of his children who interest him are the ones that present an attractive image; one daughter was especially beautiful when she was born and became his obsession for two years; he took endless photos of her. When she outgrew her babyish cuteness, he "dropped" her as an object of fascination and then immersed himself in a new obsession—competitive running. But a couple of years later, when he gained thirty pounds and had stopped jogging, he stopped talking to family about the importance of health and fitness. The subject no longer "felt good" any more.

His son was, at that time, doing Iron Man Triathlons himself, but the young man knew that fitness had now become a "taboo" subject with his father, and that if he talked to him about his own success, hearing about it would somehow make his father feel bad. Besides, John had now moved on to a new obsession that was dominating every moment of his life—building an experimental airplane. He sent pictures of every phase of the new project to every person on his email "contacts" list, most of whom, tired of John's self-absorption, simply deleted the photos without opening them.

## Janie — a "Giving / Extroverted" Narcissist: "The Cat"

Janie doesn't have naturally good facial features, but she takes advantage of every beauty technique in the book to make a stunning impression on people. She dresses like a fashion model, and it takes her an hour to put on her makeup just to go out for dinner at a hamburger joint. When you first meet Janie, she is charming and seems very interested in you. When she shows up at your house as your dinner guest, she will be dressed "to the nines" and will be holding an extravagant bouquet for you, whose wonders she will spend ten minutes telling you about, before she relinquishes it to you.

Janie will also laugh heartily at all your jokes, will drink heartily (you needn't feel bad if you get a bit drunk, because she will match you, glass for glass) and you will be sure that you have found a charming new friend to invite to your cocktail parties.

But as you get to know Janie better, you will realize that it is your "job" to make her feel good about herself. She does not have conversations with people, she "holds court" with long monologues. Even the men in the group will be forced to listen to a long, detailed story about the bargain-priced makeup she just snagged at Costco. In fact, these aren't so much conversations, as self-talk; one gets the impression that Janie is a big Persian cat, rubbing herself on your leg in order to feel good. She pauses at appropriate moments in this self-talk to wait for your praise.

Janie is glamorous, fun-loving, and accomplished; her smile is made for the camera—tightly drawn back, with teeth tapped together just at their tips, Hollywood-style. When you are invited to her house for dinner, no matter how far you have driven and how tired and hungry you are, before you are offered a drink or a chair in which to rest, you will first be given "the tour," with your job being to admire her new home decor.

If you neglect to praise her living-room color scheme or choice of artwork, her husband (who knows his own role well, after years of living with Janie) will dutifully prompt you to do so. You will see a whole room of photos, which give the immediate impression of a close-knit family circle, but you will only hear about the son who is a lawyer (he is gay, but she will not mention that), and not the angry daughter who never calls home. A second son, Tom, is "in" with Janie right now (he has no career, which previously put him "out" with her), but he has just married a girl from Italy, and Janie recently developed a fascination with all things Italian (before that, it was "all things French"), so Tom is now the person she talks about to visitors.

Janie has been married four times, always to a star-struck man whom she can control. Her children know that, despite intermittent lavish displays of attention and reassurances of their specialness, the relationship is ultimately about how they make her feel. The gay son still has a hostile-dependent entanglement with her and calls her every weekend; he knows that she both "adores" him and sees him as "special," yet doesn't (and never did) truly "see" him as a man. The other two children rarely call home.

## When Narcissists Become Parents

It is very hard for a narcissist to be a good parent to a child who is less than picture-perfect. The parent's point of view of self-reference causes the child to grow up distrusting his own perceptions, because his perceptions were never accurately reflected or "mirrored" as they should have been, by the parent. All the child's assertions were therefore presented tentatively, subject to the parent's response.

Children of severely narcissistic parents don't know who they are; they lack an intrinsic sense of self and they remain externally focused, continually seeking social cues to determine the validity of what they think and feel.

With a same-sex parent who is critical and shaming, the child may unconsciously reject the gender of that parent, because to claim the parent's gender would bond the child to a negative identification object. To protect his separateness and individual integrity, he must assert himself as "*other than*" the parent.

Or, when the narcissistic parent is of the opposite sex—for a boy, when she is the mother—he may never be able to develop an erotic attraction to a woman, because he perceives women as emotionally destabilizing, intrusive and emasculating. (His platonic female friends are an exception. With them, he can re-create the maternal relationship of mutual specialness.)

Such is the background of a considerable number of our homosexual, bisexual and transgendered clients, many of whom have substance-abuse or porn addiction problems which they use to manage their sense of internal disregulation.

We get suggestive illustrations of this family pattern from reading the autobiography of Chastity Bono, who first thought she was a lesbian, and later decided she was a man; and the biographies of several other public figures including actor Montgomery Clift, who was bisexual, and Olympic swimmer Greg Louganis, who is gay.

We also see this pattern illustrated in the play "Cat on a Hot Tin Roof," by Tennessee Williams, a much-celebrated homosexual playwright who was thought to be writing autobiographically.

And we see the narcissistic family vividly portrayed in the work of Eli Siegel in *Aesthetic Realism*, with his testimonies of men who left homosexuality after they recognized the damage done to their perception of the world by their own and their parent's narcissism.

Chapter Ten

# Seeking Understanding through the Arts: *Cat on a Hot Tin Roof* — a Play about the Narcissistic Family

*Without a man's "blessing"—something he did not get from his father—the play's lead character cannot become a procreative man, cannot live in truth, and cannot love a woman.*

*Cat on a Hot Tin Roof* was a Broadway play, later made into a movie starring Elizabeth Taylor and Paul Newman.

The plot is heavily autobiographical. Its author, Tennessee Williams, was homosexual. Although the homosexuality of the main character is only hinted in this play, Williams shows us that a man cannot be free to love a woman unless he has obtained the love, affirmation and blessing of another man. The play beautifully illustrates the family background so often found in the lives of homosexual men. We see a disconnected father and an over-involved, narcissistic mother. Brick's brother, Gooper, is clearly heterosexual, and identifies with the father. Brick, a more temperamentally sensitive man, failed to perceive his father's love, and grew into adulthood with his masculine love needs unmet. Thus, he feels blocked from fully loving a woman.

## The Playwright's Personal Life

Shy, sensitive and frail as a child owing to a debilitating bout with diphtheria, Tennessee Williams believed that he was a disappointment to his father, a man known for his alcoholism and violent temper. His mother, a noted Southern belle, was a strong-willed social climber; she focused her perfectionistic expectations on her son with special intensity when her marriage went sour. Thus the playwright's parents seem to have created the environment of what is known as the Classic Triadic Family System, a typical background in the life of homosexual men (*see* Chapters 12 and 15). While in college, Williams moved for a time in a heterosexual lifestyle, and had a crush on a female classmate. But he never seemed able to make himself acceptable to his fraternity brothers, who considered him shy and awkward. Eventually, he was drawn into gay relationships. He became an alcoholic and drug addict, and later died of an overdose, but not before he had concluded a remarkable artistic career during which he produced some of the greatest plays of the twentieth century, many of which were known to be autobiographical.

The plot of *Cat on a Hot Tin Roof* centers on a young man called Brick, and his overbearing and insensitive father, Big Daddy—the gruff, commanding patriarch of a Southern estate who uses material rewards as a substitute for love.

"What makes Big Daddy so big? . . . His big heart, his big belly," his family chants, and "his big money!"

All the men in the family are deficient in the life-forces that create masculinity. Those forces involve taking part in procreation, facing reality without illusions, and growing in the ability to fully and selflessly love another person.

In fact, the challenge to confront reality—that is, to resist the temptation to substitute a narcissistic universe of make-believe—is a recurring theme in the plays of Tennessee Williams. In *Cat on a Hot Tin Roof* (said to be his favorite creative work), Williams seems to be trying to work out his own struggle with reality, and with his sexuality as well.

When the story begins, we see Brick, the main character (played in the film by Paul Newman), whom critics have taken to embody Tennessee Williams himself. Brick is deficient in all the necessary elements of masculinity; he is neither realistic, procreative, nor loving. He is the boy stuck in a youthful narcissistic world, a rebel against the laws of life, who substitutes fantasy for reality, thus preserving his family's narcissistic illusions.

Yet Brick's name suggests he could be solid building material for the family empire, should he ever break free of his anger, his despair, and his illusions.

Brick's wife, Maggie (Elizabeth Taylor) calls him "Boy" or "boy of mine." He is not yet a man. He dreams of his lost past when he was a youthful athlete, and of another man, Skipper, for whom he has had a romantic fascination. Now, Brick can no longer be intimate with his wife, or hope to father children. He is stuck in replaying fantasies about Skipper, and thus is constantly drunk.

The play takes place on Big Daddy's birthday. The preceding night, Brick injured his ankle trying to jump the hurdles while drunk. Throughout the play, he is still on crutches. Asked "What were you jumping high hurdles for?" Brick answers, "Because I used to, and people like to do what they used to do after they've stopped being able to do it." (We note that Tennessee Williams, too, "used to" be able to love a woman when he was in college, but then became enmeshed in gay life and alcohol and drug abuse.)

Brick's father, Big Daddy, possesses two of the three masculine principles: the reality principle and procreation, but he is unable to truly care about other people. His reality is a harsh one (ruthless money-making). He is committed to promoting his lineage (procreation), but he is unable to truly love.

When he was young and single, Big Daddy found out that Big Mama was carrying his child. He said to her, without love or tenderness: "That's my kid, ain't it? I want that kid. I need him. He ain't going to have nobody else's name but mine. Let's get the preacher. That's what marriage is for. Family."

Big Daddy's flaw is that he does not like people. In his ruthless pursuit of success, he has become disconnected from this primary masculine principle (the ability to love). Therefore his wife, Big Mama, is also love-deprived, and because of her narcissism, she is not grounded in reality. "Truth!" Big Mama says. "Everybody keeps hollering about the truth. The truth is as dirty as lies!"

Big Mama's relationship to Brick is possessive and intrusive. Soon after the story begins, she hears the bad news that Big Daddy has terminal cancer, and she cries out: "I want Brick. Where's my Brick? Where's my *only son*?"

Her other son, Gooper, is the opposite of Brick. He is heterosexual; but he is also the son who makes a show of following his father's orders and of doing all the right things expected of him (such as keeping his wife continually pregnant with a brood of smiley-faced but malevolent children). He and his wife are not actually the obedient family members they seem to be, however, for they secretly plot to take away the family inheritance.

Gooper is a hollow male; materialistic and legalistic. Like Big Daddy, he lives a sham reality, and like Big Daddy, he cannot love. He can procreate, but his procreative power is soulless, creating not children, but unloved, wild sub-creatures who have been given dogs' names. Like animals, his children represent "a flesh-and-blood dynasty...waiting to take over." Maggie calls them "no-neck monsters" because "their fat little heads sit on their fat bodies without a bit of connection."

Gooper's wife is soulless and money-focused. She can procreate, but cannot foster genuine human life. She works to portray a picture-perfect family image in the typical narcissistic style, using her children to help take the family inheritance by parading them in an annoying series of theatrics designed to "entertain" Big Daddy and make him feel good about himself.

Brick's wife Maggie is the only sympathetic and noble person in this dysfunctional family. Her husband's withholding of love and his unrelenting cruelty toward her—while he remains obsessed with "that man" from the past, Skipper—has forced her to undergo, in her own words, "this horrible transformation" into something "hard and frantic and cruel."

The plot repeatedly returns to Brick's relationship with the mysterious and unseen Skipper. This is the man who is the unspoken source of Brick's and Maggie's marital conflict. The relationship with Skipper was intense and mutually dependent, with the suggestion of being homoerotic. But despite the devastating effect of this situation on Maggie, Brick refuses to talk about it.

## Longing for the Blessing of the Father

And so we understand that Brick, seeking the male connection he did not get from his father, has made the long-lost Skipper the special person in his life, allowing Skipper to overshadow the relationship with his wife. Without a man's affirmation—something he did not get from his father—Brick cannot become a procreative man, cannot live in truth, and cannot love a woman. So Brick wants to take masculine love from Skipper, but Skipper himself is needy for masculine love—and so he kills himself. Brick is left behind, brooding and numbing his misery in alcohol.

The final turning point in the play occurs when Big Daddy tries to have a "private conversation" with Brick. In his crude style, Big Daddy asks what is troubling his son. Revealing some glimmers of tenderness and self-giving in his time of suffering, Big Daddy says, "Boy, sometimes you worry me. Why do you drink?" Brick refuses to answer. All he can say is, "It's too painful and it's no use. We talk in circles. We have nothing to say to each other!"

Big Daddy wants to know the truth about his son's special relationship with Skipper, which he sarcastically refers to as "this great and true friendship." Brick had been devastated the night Skipper killed himself. Finding the dying man, Brick had screamed for help, but could not save his friend. Alluding to their unfulfilled need for a father's love, Brick explains his failure with a rhetorical question: "How does one drowning man help another drowning man?"

## Living with the Family's Narcissistic Illusions

Big Daddy persists, asking again, "Why do you drink?" In reply, Brick exposes the narcissistic illusions that plagued the family; "Mendacity! It's lies and liars! Not one lie, or one person. The whole thing." In deeper honesty, he adds, "That disgust with mendacity is really disgust with myself. That's why I'm a drunk. When I'm drunk, I can stand myself."

Big Daddy agrees that pretense and image do in fact characterize the family. But unlike Brick, who also saw the family's narcissistic illusions and turned it into self-hatred, Big Daddy did the opposite. He became cynical: he now just sees those illusions to be an unchangeable fact of life.

Big Daddy answers Brick: "Look at the lies I've got to put up with. Pretenses, hypocrisy! Pretending like I care for Big Mama. I haven't tolerated her in years. Church! It bores me, but I go. All those swindling lodges, social clubs, and money-grabbing auxiliaries that's got me on their number-one sucker list. Boy, *I've* lived with mendacity. Why can't you live with it?"

Brick (who dulls his own pain with alcohol) offers Big Daddy some morphine to kill the pain of his own cancer, but Big Daddy refuses because he wants to feel the truth. "It will kill the pain, but kill the senses, too. When you've got pain, at least you know you're alive. I'm not going to stupefy myself with that stuff. I want to think clear. I want to see everything and feel everything."

## Sitting in the Midst of Big Mama's Piled-Up Junk

The breakthrough occurs when father and son are standing in the basement of the house (in the "unconscious," or place of buried family memories) and surrounded by his mother's dusty collection of garishly outrageous "stuff"—statues, pieces of grotesque faux art, and broken furniture covered in cobwebs, which have been put into storage after her wild, image-obsessed decorating sprees. Big Daddy, softened by the knowledge of the approach of his death, and ready to talk about some of the truths of life, sits amidst that piled-up junk.

Brick is still looking for love. Big Daddy has given up the effort to either give or receive love, but in a moment of uncharacteristic honesty and tenderness, he says this about his life: "The truth is pain and sweat, paying bills and making love to a woman that you don't love anymore."

They begin a frank talk about Big Daddy's cancer. Now, the inevitability of his death shatters the family's narcissistic "false-happy" illusions. Their lifelong arguments at first resume, until Brick cries: "All I wanted was a father, not a boss! I wanted you to love me. We've known each other all my life, and we're strangers!"

Big Daddy recalls the broken relationship with his own father. "I was ashamed of that miserable, old tramp . . . ." Then he adds, unexpectedly, "I reckon I never loved anything as much as that lousy old tramp."

Big Daddy is, at last, open to loving his own son, which immediately links the three generations of men, and breaks through the deadening barrier of pretense. Now Big Daddy's caring, expressed for the first time, frees Brick to transform himself from a self-preoccupied alcoholic to a man alive to himself, and thus able to love; and through this transformation, he can now begin to respond to Maggie's womanhood.

Father and son, apparently for the first time in their lifetimes, cry together. In a moment of wild and joyful emotional release in the basement, Brick smashes his mother's ridiculous collection of discarded, pretentious "stuff." Throwing aside his crutches, he hobbles up the stairs, exultant with joy. Maggie sees his joy, and she tells the family that she senses new life in her body, and that the family will now continue through Brick's child.

Gooper and wife laugh sarcastically; they say they have heard the begging and pleading through the bedroom walls at night, when Brick refuses to be intimate with Maggie, so they know this story of her pregnancy cannot be true. Therefore Big Daddy's family and his inheritance, they insist, will continue only through them and their side of the family.

But Brick grabs his wife, full of joy, takes her to the bedroom, kicks the door shut, and embraces her with spontaneity and love for the first time since the play began. He exults that yes, it is true: there will soon be new life in Maggie's body.

And so the play ends.

## Chapter Eleven

# Gay Porn as Reparative Theatre

*The Reenactment of Games of Mastery to Resolve Identity Confusion*

Reparative Theory identifies two fundamentally distinct self-states in the homosexual man: the Assertive Self-State within which the client finds his true self, and the Shamed Self-State within which he lapses into his false self.

In working to overcome a gay porn addiction, the client comes to realize that in order to become sexually aroused, he must first leave his Assertive True Self and shift into a Shamed False Self. This shift happens without his conscious awareness. But when the therapist helps the client see the nature of this transition, then the fantasy nature of the attraction is exposed, which in turn diminishes the grip of his addiction, as well as his unwanted homosexuality.

The Self-State distinction we have identified finds theoretical support in the writings of psychoanalyst Joyce McDougall. In her clinical studies, she confirms our understanding of homosexual enactment as a gender-based self-reparation.

As one of the few, more or less contemporary psychoanalysts willing to study what were once called "the perversions," McDougall has investigated the central role of theatre and role-playing in "perverse" forms of sexual activity, including homosexuality.

McDougall understands "sexual theatre" to be a central feature of perverse sexual behavior, and she believes this theatrical reenactment to be rooted in a symbolic attempt to resolve a personal identity conflict. In this regard she confirms the classic psychoanalytic understanding of perverse sexual activity as being rooted in identity confusion.

Noting the repetitive-compulsive nature of these role enactments, McDougall (2000) found that while her patients complain about the constrained structure of these "erotic theatre pieces," they could not abstain from their enactment, "and [would] have to do it again and again and again." (182)

The compulsive/repetitive enactment of these rituals represents a symbolic attempt to resolve psychic conflict caused by a problematic parental message regarding the child's gender and/or sexuality. In the extreme case of transsexuals, for example, McDougall reports that her patients, in assuming an identity of the opposite sex, "felt that at last they would be recognized by the mother, and what she had always unconsciously desired for them." (McDougall, 2000, p. 186)

These erotic scenarios serve as a technique of psychic survival in that they preserve the feeling of subjective identity. As "compulsive neo-sexual inventions," they represent the best possible solution that the child, in the past, was able to find in the face of contradictory parental communications regarding gender identity and sex role:

> [T]hey come to the child or the adolescent as revelation of what his or her sexuality is, along with the sometimes painful recognition that it is somehow different from that of others: there is no awareness of choice. (McDougall, 1986, p. 21)

Further, she saw these dramatic, compulsive enactments as a way of preserving the narcissistically created self-image, in order to prevent it from disintegrating:

> Thus the act becomes a drug intended to disperse feeings of violence, as well as a threatened loss of ego boundaries, and a feeling of inner death.
>
> Meanwhile the partner and the sexual scenario become containers for dangerous parts of the individual. These will subsequently be mastered, in illusory fashion, by gaining erotic control over the other, or through a game of mastery within the sexual scenario. (McDougall, 1986, p. 21)

---

## References

McDougall, J., Modell, A. and Meadow, P. (2000) "Sexuality Reconsidered: a Panel Discussion." *Modern Psychoanalysis*, 25:181-189.

McDougall, Joyce (1986) "Identifications, Neo-needs and Neo-sexualities," *International Journal of Psychoanalysis*, 67:19-30.

Nicolosi, Joseph (2009) *Shame and Attachment Loss: The Practical Work of Reparative Therapy.* Downers Grove, IL: InterVarsity Press.

## Chapter Twelve

# The Homosexually Oriented Man's Relationship to Women

*Same-sex attracted men are typically too open to women, and in an unhealthy way.*

The focus of reparative therapy is not on sex, but on healing the man's distorted way of relating to other males. A reparative therapist strongly encourages the establishment of healthy, non-erotic male friendships.

There comes a time, however, when some clients complete this phase of work and express a readiness to enter an intimate relationship with a woman. This readiness must be expressed by the client himself, and cannot be encouraged by the therapist in the same way we would urge a client to seek out male friendships.

Any future success with women *will not endure*, however, without the continuation of the client's ongoing, satisfying male relationships.

To understand the particular challenges of the homosexually oriented man in his relationship to women, we must first begin by understanding the "classic triadic relationship" which is seen so very frequently in the history of our clients. This triadic relationship throws the boy on the side of the mother, with father isolated from his wife and son. The boy's father remains a mystery, while his mother is all too well known.

This misalignment gives the boy a distorted perspective of himself in relation to the masculine and the feminine. It also distorts his appreciation for the significance of gender.

In life, men and women are always challenged to try to understand each other. Straight men are often accused of failing to meet this challenge, and it is said that they are typically insensitive to women. Paradoxically, however, it is the same *lack* of sensitivity to a woman which allows the heterosexual man to develop an intimate relationship with her. He is not so attuned to females that he overreacts and loses himself in response to their needs. *To the straight man, women are mysteries,* but this is the price the he must pay for the development of his heterosexuality.

If the straight man can be faulted for insensitivity, the homosexual man can be faulted for being too reactive to women and emotionally over-involved with them. Said one homosexual client as he reviewed his failed attempts at dating women: "I have learned to be too open to women in an unhealthy way." Growing up, he had been too intensely enmeshed with his mother and become entangled by her changing emotions. She was openly disappointed and angry with his father, so as her closest confidante, he had felt responsible for filling the emotional void.

Mothers want a compliant, well-behaved, good little boy. The boy in the triadic relationship with his parents offers this appealing image of the good boy to please his mother—behind which image, however, he hides his true self. He becomes the good little boy on the outside, but on the inside, he remains intensely confused about his needs and his identity as being separate and different from that of his mother.

As the client approaches the challenge of an intimate adult relationship with a woman, this drama of the early relationship with the mother will be re-enacted.

## Falling into the Trap of a False Self

For the man with a homosexual background, the challenge is to enter into a relationship with a woman while maintaining his sense of self-possession. The job of the therapist is to monitor the client's internal sense of self as he approaches the woman. The therapist keeps the client honest with himself and prevents him from falling into the false self, which he will easily do as he did in his childhood. While there may be numerous versions, the typical false selves that emerge in a relationship with a woman are:

1. The passive-compliant.
2. The theatrical entertainer.
3. The empathic counselor.

The therapist is watching for the client's tendency to abandon himself and slip into one of those false selves when he is with her. By becoming too anxious about the woman's expectations for him, he abandons all of his needs and desires for her needs, thus losing his self-reference and reverting into the role of the entertainer, the sympathetic confidante, or the good little boy.

## Trust

The successful shift to heterosexual marriage is all about trust: "Can I trust this woman with my feelings? Will she manipulate and confuse me? Will she fail to see me for who I am, and smother me with her expectations? Will she act like she cares for me but really use me or try to control me? *In this relationship, will I be able to be myself?"*

The role of the therapist is to listen for the man's compromises of selfhood.

## The Ongoing Need for Male Friendships

No matter how successful his relationship with his wife, the man with the homosexual background will always need to have good male friendships. Many wives—even those wives who did not know that their husbands had a homosexual problem—have told me that when their husbands spend time with their male friends, they are happier and more attentive at home, and more emotionally available to them and the children. But when their husbands shrink from the challenge of men and fail to maintain those friendships, they become withdrawn, moody and emotionally unavailable to them and the children.

The married man with a homosexual background often finds conjugal relations with his wife to be less intense and exciting than they were with men. However, as a husband participating in the goodness and rightness of male-female creation, he is left with a sense of contentment and well-being. Rather than feeling depleted and depressed after sex (as he felt shortly after the adrenaline "zap" of homosexual eroticism), he is now renewed and feels satisfied and good about himself, as he experiences himself to be a true participant in the gendered world.

## Chapter Thirteen

# Why Reveal the Dark Side of the Gay Movement?

> *No one wants to be the bearer of bad news about a group that has suffered discrimination. But because homosexuality is rooted in a gender wound, the dark side of gay life keeps stubbornly emerging, in spite of public-relations efforts to submerge it.*

Statistics tell us that gay sex is often tied to substance abuse, promiscuity and unsafe sex practices. A significant proportion of gay men also participate in sadomasochism, public sex in bathhouses, and group sex.

Many people, both gay and straight, become curious about this "dark side of life" and briefly dabble in it. Soon, however, those people who are psychologically and spiritually healthier will come to reject these activities as degrading, destructive of their integrity as human beings, and "not who I am." But why, then, do some men—in fact, so many in the gay population—continue to engage in those soul-destroying obsessions and behaviors?

This phenomenon is not restricted to a fringe of the gay subculture. Even social commentator and author Andrew Sullivan—who identifies himself as a Catholic (despite his obvious rejection of foundational Catholic beliefs), and is a conservative of sorts in the gay movement—defends what he calls the "the beauty and mystery and spirituality of sex, even anonymous sex" in his book *Love Undetectable.*

And in a speech to a gathering of college students, the Reverend Mel White was also reported by *Pastoral Care Ministries Newsletter* (Spring, 2000) to have said that he does not "struggle" with pornography, but uses it. This man, in the role of a spiritual leader, is the head of Soulforce, a gay group that pickets Protestant denominational meetings to push for the blessing of same-sex unions. I have never heard of a "straight" pastor encouraging the use of pornography, especially to young people. One cannot help but think that Rev. White's immersion in gay life has had a soul-deadening effect on him.

Writers Gabriel Rotello (author of *Sexual Ecology*) and Michelangelo Signorile (*Life Outside*) are both conservatives in the sense that they have spoken out strongly about the dangers of irresponsible sex and sexually transmitted diseases, and have taken rancorous criticism from the gay community's more radical faction. Yet when Signorile speaks of the "raunchy, impersonal atmosphere" of sex in public parks and bathrooms, he is careful to note that he, himself, would never negatively judge it: "*There's nothing morally wrong with this—and I say that as someone who has certainly had my share of hot public sex, beginning when I was a teenager and well into my adulthood.*"[1]

Similarly, Gabriel Rotello says he has been maligned for his role as a so-called "moralistic crusader" against unsafe sex. Yet he explains: "Let me simply say that I have no moral objection to promiscuity, provided it doesn't lead to massive epidemics of fatal diseases. I enjoyed the '70s, I didn't think there was anything morally wrong with the lifestyle of the baths. I believe that for many people, promiscuity can be meaningful, liberating and fun." [2]

## Taking a Closer Look

When The National Association of Research and Therapy of Homosexuality (NARTH) describes the dark side of the gay movement, this is not done for the purpose of gay bashing. The primary purpose is to identify and understand a psychological pattern.

Mainstream psychologists are usually too conflicted (or simply uninformed; but more often, afraid of being called "judgmental" or "moralistic") to acknowledge any pattern or assign any significance to this sexual radicalism.

Indeed, much of the language of psychologists has been purged of evaluative judgment that could explain the meaning and significance of a particular behavior. A 1975 *Dictionary of Psychology* states that "fetishism, homosexuality, exhibitionism, sadism and masochism are the most common types of perversion." Then, 25 years later, the word "perversion" was no longer used for any of those conditions; they are known as "deviations" or "variations," so as to be stripped of any moral connotation.

## Emotional Deficits Become Sexual Fixations

But because homosexuality is deficit-based, the dark side of gay life—characterized by sexual addictions and fixations—keeps stubbornly emerging, in spite of public-relations efforts to submerge it.

*Culture Facts,* an online publication of Family Research Council, reported on a street fair that illustrates this paradox. The fair was sponsored in part by the Human Rights Campaign (HRC) and National Gay and Lesbian Task Force (NGLTF)—two very heavily funded groups committed to normalizing homosexuality in every aspect of culture.

Yet that mainstream (in gay life) event featured public whippings, body piercing, public sex, sado-masochism, and public nakedness by parade marchers. Fair booths sold bumper stickers that said, "God masturbates," and "I Worship Satan," and merchants peddled studded dog collars and leather whips (not for their dogs). On the sidelines of the public fair, a man dressed as a Catholic nun was strapped to a cross with his buttocks exposed, and onlookers were invited to whip him for a two-dollar donation.

How long can psychologists be in denial about the significance of the dark side, and ignore what it implies about the homosexual condition?

And how long will psychologists eagerly throw open the door to gay life for every sexually confused teenager?

---

### Endnotes

[1] Signorile, M. (1998), "Nostalgia trip," *The Gay and Lesbian Review* 5, No. 2, p. 27.

[2] Rotello, G. (1998) "This is sexual ecology," T*he Gay and Lesbian Review* 5, No. 2, p. 24.

## Chapter Fourteen

# What Freud Really Said About Homosexuality —and Why

*In the controversy over the normality and associated treatment success of male homosexuality, Freud's own words have been exploited by both sides of the debate.*

*That it is so easy to "lift" Freudian quotes to support opposite sides of the debate is partially due to the man's own uncertainty and ambiguity on the subject. Throughout his life, Freud approached the subject with caution, and made only tentative assumptions.*

### Freud's Ambivalence

Gay-affirmative apologists, in order to support their view of homosexuality as normal, refer to Freud's "Letter to an American Mother," in which he says that "Homosexuality . . . is nothing to be ashamed of, no vice, no degradation, it cannot be classified as an illness: we consider it to be a variation of the sexual function." However, gay-affirmative apologists omit the telling, final passage of the letter, which states: "[Homosexuality] is produced by a certain arrest of sexual development." (Freud, 2014d, p. 786)

Any sincere attempt to gain an understanding of homosexuality necessitates an inquiry into the classical psychoanalysis of Freud and his followers, who offered the first penetrating analysis of homosexuality's origins and consequences.

And of course this inquiry must begin with Freud himself. As the founder of psychoanalysis, Freud laid the foundation for more than a century of scientific investigation. From this historical context, we ask the reader to consider that critical-sounding and even deprecatory concepts and vocabulary must be understood from that perspective.

Over the course of his life, Freud expressed various ideas about homosexuality, which, beginning in 1905, he sometimes referred to as "inversion." (Freud, 2014c, p. 136) Some of Freud's statements were fragmented, incomplete, and even self-contradictory (Lewes, 1988). At times he implied that homosexuality was an illness, while at other times merely a "variation of the sexual function" caused by "an arrest in sexual development." (Freud, 1951, p. 786)

## Narcissism and Difficulties in Regulation of Self-Esteem

Freud considered homosexuality to be a perversion in the classical psychoanalytic sense of that term—*i.e.*, a condition that includes self-object limitations, narcissism, and an underdeveloped superego. (Freud, 2014)

While he thought homosexuality to be one of the "perversions," which he defined as deviations from "the normal sexual aim . . . regarded as being the union of the genitals in the act known as copulation," (Freud, 2014c, p. 46) he also made impassioned arguments for the higher human achievements accomplished by homosexuals, pointing to da Vinci and Michelangelo in particular. (Freud, 1932)

Freud strongly opposed social intolerance of homosexuals. He wrote:

> It is one of the obvious social injustices that the standard of civilization should demand from everyone the same sexual life-conduct which can be followed without any difficulty by some people, thanks to their organization, but which

> imposes the heaviest psychical sacrifices on others. (Freud, 1959a, p. 192)

At the same time, he took what some would call a moralistic view, stating that sodomy was "ethically objectionable," "loathsome" and "degrading":

> What are known as the perverse forms of intercourse... in which other parts of the body take over the role of the genitals, have undoubtedly increased in social importance. These activities cannot, however, be regarded as being as harmless as analogous extensions [of the sexual drive] in love relationships. They are ethically objectionable, for they degrade the relationships of love between two human beings from a serious matter to a convenient game, attended by no risk and no spiritual participation. (Freud, 1959a, p. 200)

In addition, Freud's intended professional, scientific views were sometimes accompanied by his personal sentiments. For example, Freud wrote three essays on the theory of sexuality in 1905, where he stated that "We never regard the genitals themselves . . . as really 'beautiful.'" (Freud, 2014c, p. 155)

In 1910, Freud wrote "Leonardo da Vinci and a Memory of His Childhood," where he describes fellatio as "a loathsome sexual perversion." (Freud, 1932, p. 86)

Freud was unclear about whether homosexual object-choice should be considered a singular and unitary entity, or several, separate varieties. (Freud, 1932, p. 101) In other words, Freud was not sure if homosexuality was a singular phenomenon or had various manifestations. He continually returned to the question of causation, offering several theories but never diverging very far from his foundational theory of the Oedipus Complex.

## The Oedipus Complex

According to Freud, the Oedipus Complex occurs within the phallic stage of a boy's psychosexual development (ages 3–6 years), during which time the mother becomes the object of her son's infantile libidinal energy (sexual desire). Because the father is the one who is privileged to sleep with his mother, the boy is propelled into an emotional rivalry with his father. To facilitate union with the mother, the boy's "id"-driven (*i.e.*, purely emotional) impulse prompts the wish to kill the father (as did Oedipus), but the boy's more pragmatic ego, in light of the reality principle, knows that the father is stronger. The boy thus remains strongly ambivalent about his father's place in the family. Fear of "castration" (the father's ability to render him powerless) eventually prompts abandonment of this death wish towards the father and the boy instead identifies with him. The resolution of the conflict between the drives of the id and the ego is the defense mechanism of identification through which the boy internalizes the personality characteristics and the masculinity of the father. In identifying with the aggressor, the boy diminishes his castration anxiety and defends himself from the father's wrath as the two contend for the mother.

The boy's identification with the father is the successful resolution of the id-ego conflict, which in turn leads to the formation of a mature sexual identity—in other words, heterosexuality. Failure to successfully resolve the Oedipus Complex fixates the boy's identification with the mother, directing his libidinal cathexis onto the father. This negative Oedipal outcome will likely result in adult homosexuality.

## The Limitations of the Oedipus Theory

One of the limitations of the Oedipus Complex theory as an explanation for homosexuality is Freud's presupposition that the Oedipus Complex is the central phenomenon in the developmental period of early childhood. Freud used the Oedipus Complex alone to explain child development and attempted to explain homosexuality with that model solely. In this model, it is the boy's successful resolution of the Oedipus Complex (*i.e.*, an inevitable competition with his father for the love of his mother) that transitions the child from auto-eroticism and narcissism into true object-relatedness and heterosexuality. Homosexuality is seen by Freud as the result of a failed resolution of the Oedipus Complex. This could occur either when this complex was not worked-through completely, or because a previous trauma had caused a psychosocial fixation within the pre-Oedipal state, preventing the child from beginning the Oedipal dynamics. (Freud, 2014c, p. 242)

An additional limitation of the Oedipus Complex model is that it views the parent-child bond as a sexually based attachment, *i.e.*, libidinal cathexis, rather than an emotional-identification bond. (Freud, 2014b, p. 174) An example of the Oedipal model's narrowness is found in Freud's attempt to explain same-sex attraction in erotic, rather than identification terms. He was clear about the boy's over-identification with the mother, but believed that this identification was due to libidinal attachment, and so he could not account for how the father then becomes a sexual object. His best explanation was that the child who becomes homosexual identifies with the mother and therefore loves men as she would. (Freud, 2014c, p. 145 n.) These limitations restricted Freud's consideration of self-identity and especially gender identity, which would be described more fully by later clinicians in self-psychology and object-relations theory.

### Resolving Freud's Ambiguities in the Hindsight of Theoretical Advances

While Freud wrote no major work exclusively dedicated to the subject, his views on the topic of homosexuality appear in diverse papers, notably "Three Essays on the Theory of Sexuality" (2014c); "Some Neurotic Mechanisms in Jealousy, Paranoia and Homosexuality" (2014g); and "Leonardo da Vinci and a Memory of His Childhood" (1932). From these three essential and other peripheral writings, his diverse views on homosexuality can be summarized from several perspectives:

### Freud's Philosophical Foundation: "The Reality of Reproduction"

Freud began his investigation of homosexuality with the assumption that biological complementarity is the basis of normal sexuality—what Rado would later term Freud's "standard pattern" (Rado, 1940, p. 464) of male-female sexual relationship. Central to this pattern is the potential for reproduction. Based on nineteenth-century biological theories and Darwinism, Freud's theory saw the role of sexual activity as the union of the genitals of members of the opposite sex for the purpose of continuing the race. (Rado, 1940, p. 464)

Summarizing this view, Arlow (1986) states that "for Freud the question of what should be considered normal as opposed to perverse sexuality posed no particular problem. He used a biological criterion." (249)

Basing his definition of "perversion" on the biological reality of reproduction, Freud stated in 1920: "The common characteristic of all perversions, on the other hand, is that they have abandoned reproduction as their aim. We term sexual activity perverse when it has renounced the aim of reproduction and follows the pursuit of pleasure as an independent goal." (Freud, 1955, p. 273)

Gay-affirmative apologists claim that Freud's fundamental criterion of procreation is archaic and unnecessary. They regard this criterion of procreation as overly simplistic and narrow, and propose instead that the aim of sexuality can be simply pleasure and relational intimacy. In so doing, the gay-affirmative apologists join the contemporary trend among therapists and theoreticians in the mental-health professions to substitute the individual's subjective experience for an objective model of health.

By equating Freud's teleological (biological design-based) principle to a moralistic principle, gay-affirmative apologists have shifted the object of study from biological design to the person's own subjective experience of meaning. This effectively moved psychoanalytic theory away from the objectivity of the natural sciences upon which Freud had attempted to build psychoanalysis. These theoretical departures from the reproductive function of sexual activity to the subjective and qualitative experience of human sexual relations served to further divide psychoanalysis from the natural sciences.

## The Theory of Universal Bisexuality

Freud's theory of universal bisexuality remained a fundamental, if problematic principle of psychoanalysis until 1940, when Sandor Rado (1940) decisively challenged that assumption. Freud thought that homosexuality was rooted not only in the unsuccessful resolution of the Oedipal Complex, but also in some undiscovered biological component that predisposes some children to homosexuality. Freud assumed that there exists either inborn (as in prenatal-hormonal) or genetic potential for homosexuality prior to the environmental events of the child's psychosexual development. Freud considered that narcissism also might have a biological component.

Describing the evolutionary basis of sexuality, Freud wrote:

> Psychoanalysis considers that a choice of an object independently of its sex—freedom to range equally over male and female objects—as it is found in childhood, in primitive states of society and early periods of history, is the original basis from which, as a result of restriction in one direction or the other, both the normal and the inverted types develop. Thus from the point of view of psychoanalysis the exclusive sexual interest felt by men for women is also a problem that needs elucidating and is not a self-evident fact based upon an attraction that is ultimately of a chemical nature. (Freud, 2014c, p. 144)

Gay-affirmative apologists have turned to Freud's theory of universal bisexuality to attempt to deconstruct his belief that the fundamental requirement of healthy sexual development must be genital functioning in the service of reproduction. These theorists argue that whether the individual uses his sexuality for reproduction or pleasure, this should not be the gauge of his psychosexual maturity.

Rado (1940) rejected Freud's notion of universal bisexuality and traced that idea to the pre-scientific mythologies of hermaphrodites and animism. He concluded that homosexuality finds its origins in childhood anxieties and not in biological constitution. Returning, like Freud, to the reproductive system as the criterion for normal sexuality, Rado claimed that Freud's theory of universal bisexuality overlooked the obvious reparative function of same-sex behavior.

## Psychosexual Immaturity

In spite of his theory of universal bisexuality, Freud viewed normal psychosexual development as inevitably ending in heterosexuality. Homosexuality represented an inhibition in development and did not represent mature sexuality. (2014c, p. 145–47, n.) The cause for this inhibition, he maintained, could be found in constitutional and early family factors.

Anticipating the release of the 1962 Bieber, *et al.* study by over fifty years, Freud summarized his understanding of the familial causes of homosexuality:

> In all our male homosexual cases the subjects had had a very intense erotic attachment to a female person, as a rule their mother . . . . This attachment was evoked or encouraged by too much tenderness on the part of the mother herself, and further reinforced by the small part played by the father during their childhood. Indeed, it almost seems as though the presence of a strong father would ensure that the son made the correct decision in his choice of object, namely someone of the opposite sex. (Freud, 1932, p. 99)

Despite his lifelong vacillation on some aspects of homosexuality, Freud maintained the consistent view that homosexuality results only when normal and natural heterosexual development is thwarted. His premise was that if the child's psychosexual development is not derailed, or if there is not some constitutional predetermination, the child will naturally attain a heterosexual object-choice.

Throughout his life, Freud's writing on homosexuality shows that he consistently understood homosexuality as an unresolved fixation, and not simply a "preference" based upon free choice. He held that homosexuality is a derailment from the natural sexual object. Freud explained that "any established aberration from normal sexuality" was "an instance of developmental inhibition and infantilism." (Freud, 2014c, p. 231) Regarding causation of homosexuality, he later wrote that "sexual aberration in adults—perversion, fetishism, inversion (homosexuality) . . . will reveal an event such as I have suggested, leading to a fixation in childhood." (Freud, 2014a, p. 182)

Freud also wrote that "perverse sexuality, in brief, is nothing more than infantile sexuality divided into its separate tendencies." (Freud, 1920, p. 268) Finally, Freud cites homosexuality as an example of "an inhibition in development." (Freud, 2014c, p. 208)

## Homosexuality and Narcissism

From his earliest formulations on the nature of homosexuality, Freud recognized the narcissistic structure of the condition: "Homosexual object-choice originally lies closer to narcissism than does the heterosexual kind." (Freud, 2014e, p. 426) He conceptualized homosexuality as a developmental mid-point between immature narcissism and mature heterosexuality (Freud, 1958). According to Freud, this mid-phase of narcissism "seeks for the subject's own ego and finds it again in other people." (Freud, 2014c, p. 222 n.)

The narcissistic nature of a boy's same-sex, sexual-object choices is first established within his identification with the mother. (Freud, 1932) This narcissistic identification with her remains an impediment to authentic relationships in adulthood.

While Freud wrote his ideas on homosexuality in scattered form, his paper on Leonardo da Vinci (1932) may be considered the most insightful and detailed analysis of the homosexual condition. In this paper, for the first time, Freud linked this inhibition in development to narcissism:

> [The homosexual] finds the objects of his love along the path of narcissism, as we say: for Narcissus, according to the Greek legend, was a youth who preferred his own reflection to everything else and who was changed into the lovely flower of that name. (Freud, 1932, p.100)

Detailing the narcissistic component in homosexuality, Freud stated:

> We have discovered, especially clearly in people whose libidinal development has suffered some disturbance, such as perverts and homosexuals, that in their later choice of love-objects they have taken as a model not their mother but their own selves. They are plainly seeking themselves as a love-object, and are exhibiting a type of object-choice which must be termed 'narcissistic.' In this observation we have the strongest of the reasons which have led us to adopt the hypothesis of narcissism. (Freud, 2014f, p. 88)

Detailing the forms of narcissistic attachment, Freud stated:

> A man can love himself as he is, he can love himself as he was, he can love someone who was once a part of himself, and he can love what he himself would like to be." (2014f, p. 90) Elaborating on this last type of love, Freud described the "impoverished" person who loves someone who possesses excellences he himself never had." (2014f, p. 101)

## Reparative Concept

The narcissistic component of homosexuality is further explained as the "satisfaction" (2014c, p. 222) that is sought in reparation for ego-wounding. The ego seeks some kind of repayment for an offense suffered, or for a perceived loss or defect. This compensatory function of the ego came to be understood in terms of narcissism.

Freud viewed homosexual behavior as a mechanism used as a defense against anxiety and fear. Earlier, Freud noted the reparative function of homosexuality in describing it as a defense against fear of women: "Their compulsive longing for men has turned out to be determined by their ceaseless flight from women." (Freud, 1932, p. 43)

Offering a clinical example of the reparative function of same-sex behavior, Freud stated:

> In the history of homosexuals one often hears that the change in them took place after the mother had praised another boy and set him up as a model. The tendency to a narcissistic object-choice was thus stimulated, and after a short phase of keen jealousy, the rival became a love-object. (Freud, 2014g, p. 232)

## Therapeutic Pessimism

Freud often expressed pessimism about the treatment of homosexuality, not because he was opposed to it in principle, but because he judged that the techniques of the time were ineffective. He explained:

> In general, to undertake to convert a fully developed homosexual into a heterosexual does not offer much more prospect of success than the reverse, except that for good practical reasons the latter is never attempted. The number of successes achieved by psychoanalytic treatment of the various forms of homosexuality, which incidentally are manifold, is indeed not very striking. (Freud, 1955, pp.150–151)

Another reason Freud was pessimistic about treatment was that he saw the homosexual as a pervert (in the psychoanalytic sense) rather than a neurotic. Typically, the neurotic was sufficiently enough distressed by his symptoms to be motivated to seek professional help. Because he experienced anxiety regarding his symptoms, he developed a transference onto the therapist, which is necessary for psychoanalytic treatment success. On the other hand, the "pervert" was thought to feel no internal conflict and gained too much ego-pleasure from his behavior.

As Freud wrote, "Perverts who can obtain satisfaction do not often have occasion to come for analysis." (Freud, 2014a, p. 197)

Freud later explained:

> The homosexual is not able to give up the object that provides him with pleasure, and one cannot convince him that if he made the change he would rediscover in the other the pleasure that he has renounced. If he comes to be treated at all, it is mostly through the pressure of external motives, such as the social disadvantages and dangers attaching to his choice of object, and such components of the instinct of self-preservation prove themselves too weak in the struggle against the sexual impulsions. One then soon discovers his secret plan, namely, to obtain from the striking failure of his attempt a feeling of satisfaction that he has done everything possible against his abnormality, to which he can now resign himself with an easy conscience. (Freud, 1955, p. 150)

Freud found that most homosexuals entered treatment due to "external motives, such as social disadvantages and danger attaching to his choice of object," (Freud, 1955, p. 151) but that his true motivation was not to be cured, per se, but rather to avoid social criticism, and to assure himself that he tried his best to change and "can now resign himself with an easy conscience" to his sexual pleasure. (Freud, 1955, p. 150) This, and the belief that homosexuality was in part due to biological predisposition, apparently were the causes for Freud's pessimism.

While Freud was pessimistic about treatment success, he did not exclude the possibility of change, but rather thought that psychoanalysis could offer the patient a more conflict-free adjustment to his homosexuality. Thus, Freud wrote:

> It is not for psychoanalysis to solve the problem of homosexuality. It must rest content with disclosing the psychical mechanisms that resulted in determining the object-choice, and with tracing back the paths from them to the instinctual dispositions. There its work ends, and it leaves the rest to biological research. (Freud, 1955, p. 171)

This limited perspective is illustrated by his response to a mother who hoped Freud could cure her son of his homosexuality:

> What analysis can do for your son runs in a different line. If he is unhappy, neurotic, torn by conflicts, inhibited in his social life, analysis may bring him harmony, peace of mind, full efficiency, whether he remains a homosexual or gets changed. (Freud, 2014d, p. 786)

Since those early years, psychoanalysis has developed a more refined distinction between the neurotic and the pervert, as well as techniques to counter resistance in therapy. For example, Socarides and Freedman (2002) thought that confronting the patient's denial of reality would create sufficient intrapsychic conflict to lay the foundation for the therapeutic alliance. Similarly, Chasseguet-Smirgel (1974) was hopeful in believing that "there exists in the sexual pervert's mind a more reality-oriented ego-ideal which is revealed in analysis." (351) Cultivating these reality-oriented aspects of the patient's mind, along with other efforts, have brought more positive reports of treatment since Freud's time.

## Homosexuality as Perversion

While the term "perversion" today has taken on a pejorative connotation, we need to consider the historical context in which Freud intended the use of the term. Socarides tells us that "while Freud himself deplored the word 'perversion' because it carried a moralistic connotation, he continued to use it free from its pejorative meaning and in a scientific sense. He used it to denote sexual arousal patterns that are unconsciously motivated, stereotyped, and derived from early psychic conflict." (Socarides, 2002, p. 5)

In addition, Freud cautioned that it is difficult, if not impossible, to draw a clear distinction between "mere variations" and "pathological symptoms."

> No healthy person, it appears, can fail to make some addition that might be called perverse to the normal sexual aim; and the universality of this finding is in itself enough to show how inappropriate it is to use the word perversion as a term of reproach. In the sphere of sexual life we are brought up against peculiar and, indeed, insoluble difficulties as soon as we try to draw a sharp line to distinguish mere variations within the range of what is physiological from pathological symptoms. (Freud, 1905/1949, p. 39)

For Freud, the term perversion should be understood "in the content of the new sexual aim . . . in its relation to the normal." (Freud, 1949, p. 39) "The normal," for Freud, remains "the biological reality of reproduction." (Freud, 1955)

The point at which a child became fixated in his psychosexual development determined whether or not he suffered from a perversion. The etiology of homosexuality placed the fixation before the period of the Oedipal Conflict, making the condition a perversion. One characteristic of the perversions is the attempt to master anxieties by excessive erotic investment in the "loved" object, *i.e.,* libidinization. This, in turn, leads to a disturbance in the patient's relationship to reality.

Success in mastering the Oedipal conflict allows the boy to move beyond the narcissistic phase of development, with its more primitive need-gratifying object relations, to a maturity that allows true object-relatedness. When the boy successfully navigates the Oedipal period, his identification with the father allows him to develop an authentic connectedness with social reality, a healthy superego, and the ability to internalize social/moral and aesthetic norms.

The homosexual's continuing focus upon narcissistic object choices restricts his ability to establish a mature sexuality based upon healthy object relations. This focus on narcissistic gratification limits his sexual-object choices to those which offer reassurance against depletion of his masculinity (threats of castration). His tendency to seek an idealized object to fulfill his unmet narcissistic needs means that his relationships will be built upon psychic projections and repetitive enactments of reassurance.

## Homosexuality and Paranoia

Freud was the first to report the commonly found association between homosexuality and some degree of paranoia, which was frequently confirmed by other psychoanalysts. (Lewes, 1988) He believed that such paranoia resulted from the homosexual's inability to accept his own homosexuality. The transformative process from intolerable homosexuality to paranoia begins as follows: "I (a man) love him (another man)." This results in a reaction-formation defense mechanism, which protects him from the intolerable idea of homosexual attraction: "No, I don't love him—I hate him." The resulting paranoid delusion, therefore, is "And the reason I hate him, is that he persecutes me." (Paraphrased from Freud, 1958, p. 63.)

## Homosexuality and Healthy Personality

The fundamental question for Freud was whether homosexual love could be truly other-related; or, was it simply an extension of infantile pleasure-seeking, or an attempt at narcissistic gratification with a partial object?

He was impressed by the great artists whom he thought to be homosexual, such as da Vinci and Michelangelo, and he viewed them as some of the highest-level contributors to culture and mankind. (Freud, 1932) While Freud believed that homosexuality was an inhibition of normal psychosexual development, he recognized that it need not be an obstacle to development of the personality in other respects:

> [Homosexuality] is similarly found in people whose efficiency is unimpaired, and who are indeed distinguished by specially high intellectual development and ethical culture...[and] found in people who exhibit no other serious deviations from the normal. (Freud, 2014c, p. 35)

### The Masculine Homosexual

In addition, Freud did not see homosexuality as invariably a problem with masculinity. He thought it possible for a homosexual man to be completely masculine-identified.

He wrote, "In men, the most complete mental masculinity can be combined with inversion." (Freud, 2014c, p. 142)

Years later, Freud noted: "A man with predominantly male characteristics and also masculine in his erotic life may still be inverted in respect to his object, loving only men instead of women." (Freud, 1955, p. 170) In this respect, his views precede what Socarides later described as the post-Oedipal type of homosexuality. (Socarides, 1989; Nicolosi, 2009)

## Conclusion

Classical psychoanalysis contains substantial contributions to the understanding of homosexuality.

Recent political changes within the psychological profession have resulted in the questioning (or simple ignoring) of those conclusions. The founder of psychoanalysis proposed ideas that have since been interpreted differently by both sides of the debate, with one side claiming that Freud supported the view that homosexuality is a "normal sexual variant," while the other side asserts that he said homosexuality is a "pathological condition."

Self-serving selections of Freud's own words are easily obtainable because, as this paper has shown, Freud was ambivalent and sometimes even self-contradictory on the subject.

Nevertheless, considering the limitations of Freud's historical and cultural perspective, along with his rather narrow theoretical framework of the Oedipus complex, he was able to establish fundamental principles that have proven fruitful to psychodynamic thinking during the one hundred years since he first wrote.

These fundamental principles include the likelihood that a male homosexual experienced over-identification with his mother, and a poor relationship with his father; that narcissism is a common feature of male homosexual development; and that same-sex erotic attractions serve a reparative function.

These three principles have repeatedly been confirmed by mental-health professionals over a century of clinical practice.

## References

Arlow, J. A. (1986). Discussion of papers by Dr. McDougall and Dr. Glasser: Panel on identification in the perversions. *The International Journal of Psychoanalysis,* 67, 245–50.

Bieber, I., Dain, H., Dince, P., Drellich, M., Grand, H., Gundlach, R., Kremer, M., Rifkin, A., Wilber, C., & Bieber, T. (1962), *Homosexuality: A Psychoanalytic Study of Male Homosexuals.* New York: Basic Books.

Chasseguet-Smirgel, J. (1974), "Perversion, idealization and sublimation." *International Journal of Psychoanalysis,* 55, 349–57.

Freud, S. (1949), *Three essays on the theory of sexuality* (J. Strachey, Trans.), London, England: Imago Publishing (Original work published in 1905).

Freud, S. (1932), "Leonardo da Vinci and a memory of his childhood," in J. Strachey (Ed., Trans.), *The Standard Edition of the Complete Psychological Works of Sigmund Freud,* vol. 11, pp. 59–137, London: Hogarth Press. (Original work published in 1910).

Freud, S. (1955), "The psycho-genesis of a case of homosexuality in a woman." in J. Strachey (Ed., Trans.), *The Standard Edition of the Complete Psychological Works of Sigmund Freud,* vol. 18, pp. 145–72. London: Hogarth Press. (Original work published in 1920).

Freud, S. (1958), "Psycho-analytic notes upon an autobiographical account of a case of paranoia (dementia paranoides)," in J. Strachey (Ed., Trans.), *The Standard Edition of the Complete Psychological Works of Sigmund Freud*, vol. 12, pp. 1–84. London: Hogarth Press. (Original work published in 1911).

Freud, S. (1959a), "'Civilized' sexual morality and modern nervous illness," in J. Strachey (Ed., Trans.), *The Standard Edition of the Complete Psychological Works of Sigmund Freud,* vol. 9, pp.177–204. London: Hogarth Press. (Original work published in 1908).

Freud, S. (1959b), *Group psychology and the analysis of the ego*, J. Strachey (Ed., Trans.). New York: W.W. Norton. (Original work published in 1922).

Freud, S. (1963), "The libido theory and narcissism." In J. Strachey (Ed., Trans.), *The Standard Edition of the Complete Psychological Works of Sigmund Freud,* vol. 16, pp. 412–30. London: Hogarth Press. (Original work published in 1917).

Freud, S. (1964), "New introductory lectures on psychoanalysis," in J. Strachey (Ed.,Trans.), *The Standard Edition of the Complete Psychological Works of Sigmund Freud,* vol. 22, pp. 3–182, London: Hogarth Press. (Original work published in 1933).

Freud, S. (2014a), "A child is being beaten: A contribution to the study of the origin of sexual perversion," in J. Strachey (Ed., Trans.), *The Standard Edition of the Complete Psychological Works of Sigmund Freud,* vol. 7, pp.175–204. (Original work published in 1919.) Retrieved from Psychoanalytic Electronic Publishing. http://www.pep-web.org/index.php

Freud, S. (2014b), "The dissolution of the Oedipus Complex," in J. Strachey (Ed., Trans.), *The Standard Edition of the Complete Psychological*

*Works of Sigmund Freud*, vol. 19, pp. 171–80. (Original work published in 1924.) Retrieved from Psychoanalytic Electronic Publishing. http://www.pep-web.org/index.php

Freud, S. (2014c), "Three essays on the theory of sexuality," in J. Strachey (Ed., Trans.), *The Standard Edition of the Complete Psychological Works of Sigmund Freud*, vol. 7, pp.123–246. (Original work published in 1905.) Retrieved from Psychoanalytic Electronic Publishing. http://www.pep-web.org/index.php

Freud, S. (2014d), "Letter to an American mother," *The American Psychiatric Journal* 107, No. 10, 786–87. (Original work published in 1951.) https://ajp. psychiatryonline. org/doi/abs/ 10.1176/ajp.107.10.786

Freud, S. (2014e), "Mourning and melancholia," in J. Strachey (Ed., Trans.), *The Standard Edition of the Complete Psychological Works of Sigmund Freud*, vol. 16, pp. 237–58. (Original work published in 1917.) Retrieved from Psychoanalytic Electronic Publishing. http://www.pep-web.org/index.php

Freud, S. (2014f), "On Narcissism: an Introduction," in J. Strachey (Ed., Trans.), *The Standard Edition of the Complete Psychological Works of Sigmund Freud*, vol. 14. (Original work published in 1914.) Retrieved from Psychoanalytic Electronic Publishing. http://www.pep-web.org/index.php

Freud, S. (2014g), "Some neurotic mechanisms in jealousy, paranoia and homosexuality," in J. Strachey (Ed., Trans.), *The Standard Edition of the Complete Psychological Works of Sigmund Freud*, vol. 8, pp. 221–32. (Original work published in 1922.) Retrieved from Psychoanalytic Electronic Publishing, http://www.pep-web.org/index.php

Gershman, H. (1953), "Considerations of some aspects of homosexuality," *American Journal of Psychoanalysis* 13, pp. 82–83.

Lewes, K. (1988), *The Psychoanalytic Theory of Male Homosexuality.* New York: Simon and Schuster, p. 43.

Nicolosi, J. (2009), *Shame and Attachment Loss: The Practical Work of Reparative Therapy*. Downers Grove, Ill: InterVarsity Press.

Nunberg, H. (1938), "Homosexuality, magic and aggression." *International Journal of Psychoanalysis,* 19, pp. 1–16.

Ovesey, L. (1969), *Homosexuality and Pseudo-Homosexuality,* New York: Science House.

Pretlow, L, (2010), "The impact of neurophysiologic development on the regulation and treatment of homosexual impulses," Paper presented at the Panel Discussion on the Neurophysiology of Homosexuality at the NARTH Convention, Philadelphia, PA.

Rado, S. (1940), "A critical examination of the concept of bisexuality," *Psychosomatic Medicine* 2 (4), 459-67.

Socarides, C.W. (1989), *Homosexuality: Psychoanalytic Therapy*. New York: Jason Aronson.

Socarides, C.W, Freedman, A. (Ed.) (2002), "Advances in the psychoanalytic theory and therapy of male homosexuality," in *Objects of Desire: the Sexual Deviations*. New York: International University Press.

## Chapter Fifteen

# Lessons from the Lives of Celebrities: Montgomery Clift

*Because he cannot maintain genuine connectedness with himself or others, the child of the narcissistic family suffers from a pervasive sense that life is meaningless.*

Montgomery Clift was a leading classical actor during the heyday of Hollywood. Reading a biography of his short and tormented life, we recognize a striking example of the Triadic Narcissistic Family System, one of the features found in the backgrounds of many homosexual men.

Monty Clift portrayed an image of the sensitive, broodingly handsome hero. In spite of his fame and wealth, he led a difficult life, dying prematurely after many years of drinking, drugs and a long string of affairs with men, as well as a few with women. With his compelling screen presence, he portrayed a haunting vulnerability that was evidently as much "who he was" off-screen as on-screen.

In Clift's biography, we see an extreme example of the charming, controlling, over-involved mother, who contrasts with the withdrawn father who allows the mother to lead in every family matter. Monty, fatally, was the "good" son who did not rebel (which would have been the healthier response) and instead became the perfectionistic high-achiever his mother wanted him to be, while growing up unable to trust his own feelings and unsure of who he was.

Clift and his siblings harbored a family secret that something was very wrong behind the "perfect" family image his mother attempted to portray, but they were not sure what that "wrong thing" was. Monty, like so many other boys who grow up to be same-sex-attracted, was the compliant child, the one among the siblings who absorbed the expectations of the narcissistic parent; and he was the child whose restless drivenness and inability to trust his own feelings gradually led, in adulthood, to his own self-destruction.

## The Family Secret

A common feature of the Triadic Narcissistic family system is the existence of some unspoken secret that is kept from outsiders, and even from themselves. Beneath the normal, even "ideal" family image, there is "something wrong," something "too weird" to discuss even among siblings. Perhaps it is the secret that his parents actually didn't love each other, or else (as Montgomery Clift's siblings suspected), perhaps their parents weren't the happy people they publicly presented themselves to be.

Adult children from narcissistic family systems who enter therapy often speak to their siblings to confirm their own perception of some kind of distortion: "Was it true," they ask their brothers and sisters, "that it really happened that way?" When they do share their tentative impressions, they are often surprised to discover they shared the same, "strange" impressions. The parents' conflicting messages were too confusing to sort out, making it easier to retreat to the belief that "everything was OK."

The man from the Narcissistic Family rarely recognizes the pathology in his upbringing. At the start of therapy he may report a very normal family life—despite his inability to feel and express anger, his low self-esteem and feelings of inadequacy in relationships, his depression, cynical and pessimistic moods, and difficulty in making decisions.

There is often no obvious family dysfunction, because the malattunement was subtle, covered up, not obvious to an outsider—and deliberately hidden behind the parents' imperative to show a perfect image to the world. The less-perceptive therapist will therefore often attest that "things in the family were normal," yet the client knows that somehow, they "felt strange."

## The Allure of Theatre and Acting

The child of the Triadic-Narcissistic Family must develop a coping mechanism to survive. The homosexually developing boy typically does so by creating a False Self, which we see in his role of the "Good Little Boy." This allows him to bury his "bad" self and assume a new role which adapts to the demands of his environment. In doing so, however, he will necessarily sever his connection with his inner emotional life.

In compensation, he often develops a fascination with fantasy, theatre and acting, taking on the emotional life of someone else. If he was born with the temperamental traits of creativity and sensitivity, he will find it especially easy to retreat to the compensatory pleasure he feels in fantasy.

As Clift's brother said, when Monty played someone else, he was at last freed from his old role as the "good" son, and he no longer had to live up to the persona his mother had created for him. Without having to feel guilt for transgressing against his mother, he could at last, on the stage, wrest himself free of the "good boy" and claim the persona of another man.

As a side note, we should mention that gay men also tend to seek meaning and spiritual solace in the reality-denying and gender-blurring archetypes of New Age philosophy.

## Failure to Emotionally Connect Leads to a Sense of Existential Meaninglessness

The child of this family simply does not know himself, because his parents confused their own needs with his needs. Because the child can never fully satisfy his parents' perceived needs, he feels like a failure. He has a (correct) sense that he is inadequate, immature, unprepared for adult responsibility, and unready to assume control over his life. He continues to bend to the expectations of others. He has grown up without knowing "who 'owns' the 'should,'" because he never received accurate mirroring; that is, accurate parental attunement to who he was, as a person separate and different from his parents.

Because he cannot maintain genuine emotional connectedness with himself or others, he suffers from a pervasive sense that life is empty and meaninglessness—which of course, when he is laboring under such limitations, it is. One homosexual client explained it to me his way:

"Life is just so . . . [searching for a word] . . . *petty!*"

## Impairment of the Child's Gender Maturation

The boy who grows up within the Triadic-Narcissistic Family will also develop trust issues which center around the gendered self—*i.e.*, he will fear that men will "diminish" and "degrade" him, while women (like his mother) will manipulate and control him, and drain him of his masculine power.

In her biography of Clift, author Patricia Bosworth describes Monty's father, Bill, as passive, good-natured, and very dependent on his charismatic wife, Sunny. A successful man in the business world, Bill nevertheless would defer to this strong-willed, opinionated woman at home. "My father would do anything in the world to please Mother," Monty's sister Ethel said. (23)

She made everyone—including her husband—feel *that no one with any brains* could possibly disagree with her and still be a person of consequence." (31) Indeed, Sunny was known as a vibrantly attractive and intelligent woman. She was "energetic, sometimes venomous, always triumphant in any situation." (284)

Sunny herself had been adopted as an infant into a family that left her feeling unimportant and unloved, and she was never able to locate her birth parents. She had been told, however, that her bloodlines made her a "thoroughbred." She became obsessed with tracking down her genealogy, and she poured all her energy into it. Her primary goal in life, biographer Boswell says, was to raise her children as "the thoroughbreds they were" so they would never know the insecurity she had suffered in her life. She gave birth to two boys (Monty and Brooks) and one girl (Ethel). Sunny did not seem to respect their biological gender differences.

Monty and the others were being raised as triplets, given identical haircuts . . . clothes, lessons, and responsibilities, regardless of age or sex.

Brooks, the tougher son, rebelled—fighting and talking back to his mother when he was told he must dress like his younger brother and sister. "I wanted to be myself," he explained later. Brooks—who grew up to be straight—was married and divorced several times. However, Monty, like most sons in such a family who take a different path and grow up gay, "appeared the most docile, the most obedient of the three children. He did precisely what he was told . . . ." Biographer Bosworth notes that Monty's "independent impulses, his drives, were curbed again and again" by his mother. (31)

In spite of the intense pain the relationship brought him, Monty, his brother Brooks later recalled, "had a secretive relationship" of mutual specialness with their mother which Brooks and his sister "never intruded upon." (50) In contrast with this secret specialness, Monty had almost no relationship with his father. They "rarely communicated about anything" and in the morning, they would both read the paper while sitting at the breakfast table, "rarely exchanging a word." (55)

Isolated from other boys by his mother, the sensitive Monty developed an intense closeness to his sister Ethel. "Throughout his life Monty relied on Sister for comfort and advice . . . . Their insecurities made them inseparable. By the time they were seven they were sharing every secret, every fantasy." (26)

All three children complained that they were lonely because they weren't allowed to play with other children in the neighborhood, but Sunny never explained why: she just forbade it. When Brooks later confronted his father Bill about their isolated childhood, Bill told him that he shouldn't feel bad about it—it was for his own good—because they were special, just like their mother was:

> Everything she did for you, she did because she believes you are thoroughbreds. If only I could convince you of your mother's greatness—she is a great, great woman. She wanted you to have every advantage—and all the love she never had. (49)

## "You Be Happy, So I Can Be Happy!"

In the Clift family, there was apparently no room for anyone but Sunny to vent anger or express opinions. The father deferred to his wife to settle family disagreements, and would not defend the children. In the Clift family, as his biographer said, "Ma was always right." She would tell them that her entire life was dedicated to and sacrificed for them, so "the least they could do" was to behave, achieve, and make her happy.

Indeed, "keeping Sunny happy" was understood to be essential to holding the family together. Monty's father, on a business trip, described himself as "miserable" whenever he was away from his wife. He wrote his son a letter, reminding him who gave the Clift family its identity:

> Your mother is the heart of the Clift family. All our hopes and ambitions center around her. We love her better than all else, and we are ambitious because of her. She is the very lifeblood of the family . . . . (38)

Sunny tutored the children at home; her plan was that the children "would be beautifully educated but they would have to associate only with each other, 'with their own kind.'" (19) Their father had little influence, as he continually "came and went" between business deals in Manhattan and Chicago.

When the children were old enough to appreciate culture, Sunny took them to Europe for two years. Their father, says Clift's biographer, "had worked weekends and 14-hour-long days trying to give them the creature comforts Sunny had insisted were their right, by heritage." (22) They stayed at the best hotels, but were always expected to keep to themselves.

It was not long before the Clift brothers soon began to be cruelly teased by other boys. At times, a "mob" of boys would chase them home on their bicycles.

Then, the stock market crashed and bankrupted the family, and Bill Clift became deeply depressed. His wife, always determined to push through adversity, bolstered her husband and "gave me courage," Bill said, "when nobody else would." (35) The children later recalled that both parents tried to act as if nothing was wrong. The children continued to "sleep on silk sheets" in the dark, dingy room they rented, and no one talked about the dire change in their living arrangements.

## Hazy, Uncertain Memories

"As an adult, Monty refused to discuss his childhood with anyone—not even his closest friends," and both his brother and sister reported a similar "amnesia." "Once they left home and began living their own lives," Monty's biographer said, "they blanked out much of those years." (35) Monty's brother, Brooks, noted that:

> Psychologically we couldn't take the memories . . . so we forgot. But at the same time we were obsessed with our childhood. We'd refer to it among ourselves, but only among ourselves. Part of each of us desperately wanted to remember our past, and when we couldn't, it was frustrating. It caused us to weep, when we were drunk enough . . . . (36)

All three children felt "profound anxieties they could not comprehend," as Sunny tried harder and harder to "cast everyone in their assigned roles, and deny their individual needs." (38)

## Acting as Release from a False Role

By the age of 12, Monty had found the one love of his life—that is, becoming another person through pretense and acting. He was fascinated with theatre and with the spectacle of the circus. His brother Brooks said acting was the perfect release for Monty because when he played someone else, he was at last freed from his old role that had been created for him by his mother: "Now he no longer had to live up to the image Sunny imagined for him." (44)

## "You're Special, I'm Special"

Although Sunny was fiercely devoted to her children, on a deeper level, the relationship was clearly self-centered and narcissistically driven. Returning from an acting job one time, Monty teased his father, saying everyone thought Monty looked Jewish onscreen (his father disliked Jews). Father and son began arguing. But instead of trying to make peace between them and settle the discord, Sunny's question to her son was, "Monty, dear, why are you doing this *to me*??" (285) Says his biographer:

> The sound of that question brought back memories of his boyhood when every time he attempted to be independent—to make choices, decisions—she told him he was wrong and she was right; and when he disobeyed her anyway, she would cry, "*Why are you doing this to me?*" (285)

Monty was 18 and working in a job onstage when a fellow actor, Pat Collinge, noted something strange: Monty's male roommate had to move out and make bed space for Sunny to share her son's room whenever she visited him. "Everybody . . . thought it was rather odd," Collinge said, "for an 18-year-old boy to share his bedroom with his mother." (58) Collinge noted of Sunny, "I found her bewitching and charming, but a killer too. She stifled and repressed Monty by not allowing him to give vent to his enthusiasms or his deep needs." (58)

At 17, Monty went away for the summer but he received a phone call from his mother every day. She discouraged him from dating and told him to conserve his energy for his career.

It was not long before Monty began dating men. One of them described Monty as a "beautiful darling boy" who was "incapable of growing up." (66)

Monty slowly began to make a life apart from his mother. However, his closest lifelong female friends (most notably, Elizabeth Taylor) were very much like his mother; magnetic, strong-willed, charming and controlling women with whom he became enmeshed in intense (but platonic) relationships which allowed them both to feel important and admired. "As time passed, Monty slept with both men and women indiscriminately in an effort to discover his sexual preference, but his conflict remained obvious" (67), says his biographer.

The rest of Montgomery Clift's life was marred by alcoholism and depression. The hostile-dependent relationships he developed with platonic women friends caused him recurrent distress: "Some days he would threaten to stop seeing Elizabeth Taylor—then, the thought would make him burst into tears." (369) No doubt Clift enjoyed the sense of mutual specialness such relationships created, in a reenactment of the hostile dependency he once shared with his mother.

Eli Siegel, the poet-philosopher and founder of Esthetic Realism, says that the homosexual son feels both animosity and love toward the mother. This results in his feeling "adoring contempt" toward her. As one student of Aesthetic Realism explained, the homosexual man "robs a woman of dimension . . . he gushes over her, while he contemptuously dismisses her."

Later in his life, Clift had a near-fatal car accident when he was driving home drunk from a party, which left him with permanent facial disfigurement. This started him into a spiral of intractable depression.

The tragic death of this brilliant actor—alone at age 45 in a hotel room—was said to have been brought on by complications from longtime drug abuse and alcoholism. Yet there is no doubt that this sensitive child of a narcissistic family, growing up with all its predictable ill-effects on sexual orientation and personal individuation, had simply been unable to cope with life.

## Chapter Sixteen

# When an Ex-Gay Man Returns to a Gay Lifestyle

From time to time, well-known spokesmen for the ex-gay movement will announce their return to a gay lifestyle, followed by the media's predictable, joyful fanfare.

John Paulk is one example of a man who left his wife and three sons after more than 20 years of marriage, and rejoined the gay community. He renounced his former married life and proceeded to discourage others from attempting change.

Long ago, John emerged from a very troubled past. Prior to his Christian conversion, he assumed an identity as "Candi," a cross-dressing and drug-using prostitute, immersing himself in the wilder and more anti-social aspects of the gay world. But his Christian conversion led him into a stark change: marriage with Anne, a former lesbian and a committed Christian woman dedicated to an orthodox understanding of family and sexuality, with whom he raised three sons.

He also had a key position with the ministry Focus on the Family, where he became a well-known media figure testifying to his commitment to heterosexual family life and the traditional, Biblical understanding of sexuality, which holds that a gay identity is a false construct, not part of our human design. But later, that life crumbled.

As a reparative therapist who has worked with thousands of homosexually oriented men seeking change, I believe I am in a unique position to speculate on such events.

First, such a story is a cautionary tale about ex-gay celebrity. There is an inherent risk in the ex-gay movement's reliance on any public spokesperson.

Second, in his testimony, John advises against Reparative Therapy, but he himself was never in such therapy. Rather, he left his gay/transgender lifestyle as a result of a conversion experience to Christianity.

As John has told his own story, he is a man who always felt unloved and who always searched for identity and belonging. I will not speculate about his own interior processes, because it would not be appropriate for me to do so, and I do not know them. I will, however, speak of psychological patterns I have seen in other SSA men who have gone from "ex-gay" back to "gay" in their lifestyles. I believe there is a predictable pattern.

For many SSA men, the deepest problem they must wrestle with is not their sexual identity, but core identity. The original source of this struggle is not the more obvious problem in bonding with the father, but also, a breach in the primary attachment with the mother. For these men, their deepest-level problem is about something much more fundamental than sexuality: *identity, attachment and belonging*. Gender-identity conflict and erotic attraction to men are only surface symptoms. This is the problem that the media chooses to ignore, and which both sides of the debate fail to acknowledge.

## A Fragile and Changing Self-Identity

As such a man's identity evolves, there will be an excited "discovery of my True Self," followed by disillusionment, then a new, different, "*real* discovery of my True Self this time," and then again, another round of disillusionment. At the base of this desperate search is the anguished grasp for a stable personhood, with a profound feeling of emptiness and beneath it, a self-hatred. That self-hatred is often expressed in deconstructing and condemning every previous aspect of his own former life, including the influence of persons most near to him.

Radical shifts in "the discovery of my True Self" are associated, in many such people, with borderline personality disorder, narcissistic personality disorder and gender confusion. A fragile basic self-identity makes the later structuring of gender identity particularly perilous.

The restlessness such people feel is shown in a chronic state of dissatisfaction; in the narcissistic expectation that "if others really love me, they must take this pain away from me; and they [or what they stand for] are responsible for my pain." When others fail to do this, there is a deep sense of betrayal; betrayal that these individuals failed to take away the core emptiness, and so the person in conflict will become bitterly angry at the people who participated in his former life.

The pain of an identity search and the need for escape from the ordinariness and sameness of everyday life can be alleviated for awhile, at least, by adulation. The narcissistic inflation found in celebrity, for example, is an intoxicating balm.

This periodic disillusionment leaves behind devastated individuals who have invested deeply in the person; in John's own case, Anne, his former wife of 20 years.

The gay community wants to frame changes from ex-gay back to gay as proof that people who experience SSA were simply "born" for homosexuality, but we would be deceived if we believed this simplistic paradigm.

Where core identity is the foundational problem, we suspect an early-childhood breach in the primary attachment with the mother.

From my clinical experience, there is a particular kind of client who can be described as follows. He is deeply dissatisfied with gay life, leaves it, and eventually succeeds in developing good heterosexual functioning, at which time he decides to think of himself as "ex-gay." But he will, over time, struggle to muster the self-discipline and maturity to put in a hard day's work, come home to spouse and family, help the children with the homework, have dinner and settle down to a good conversation with his wife.

Such a life of day-to-day investment in one's loved ones just seems too confining. It is boring, lusterless, unexciting, "just not enough." Underneath the boredom and restlessness remains this deep, chronic dissatisfaction with life. He finds himself depressed. Perhaps, he thinks, I am not ex-gay after all. Perhaps it was all an illusion.

The dissatisfaction is not just about needing to find a partner of a different gender; it's about desiring attention, having the freedom to flirt and be admired, being made to feel special by others, and distracting oneself from one's chronic dissatisfaction with life through high-octane parties, such as the gay community offers on its well-known, drug-saturated, sex-on-demand party circuits.

In fact, I suspect that such "excitement" was what John was looking for when he went to the gay bar in Washington, D.C. many years ago, just after speaking at a Love Won Out conference, when he created a public-relations crisis while working for Focus on the Family. I suspect he was bored with the straight-laced Christian community and its expectations—I believe he sought flirtation, attention, admiration, an adrenaline-fueled adventure, and—a favored word in gay politics— "transgression."

There is a great deal of satisfaction in the gay party circuit that, for a brief time, seems to be the answer to life's emptiness and the limitations that family life imposes. For a time, you get to become the "star" — not having to deal with investing yourself in others, but always seeking that mysterious and exciting new man who will fill up the emptiness.

Of course, every identity shift a person makes, from "I thought I was such-and-such . . ." to "Now I *really* know who I am," will have its cheering admirers.

Who is the "real me"? The ex-gay, or the gay man? Each man must decide for himself. But as I see it, nature, and the design we are born to live out, reveals the solution that will give us peace.

## Chapter Seventeen
# The Value of Grief Work

*"Unfinished grieving" leaves its mark in a lifestyle of emotional self-protection.*

Grief Work is an important part of the psychotherapy process for a considerable number of clients. Such men will benefit from returning to revisit, from time to time, that painful, despairing place within them. The memory of not having felt authentically known and validated, with the shame that accompanies that awareness, can offer an opening into the grief experience.

Most of the clients I see have experienced a core gender-identity injury. Whenever a person has experienced an injury to the core self, revisiting the injury is so deeply unsettling that it feels like the threat of death—with the risk of total annihilation. It is emotionally agonizing and physically searing.

Perhaps 80% of the clients who came to the Thomas Aquinas Psychological Clinic have fit the model I describe, which involve a core gender-identity deficit; about 20% of cases have different histories.

In the earliest phase of Grief Work, the client is often surprised by the extent and depth of his buried pain. It is not unusual to hear him say something like, "I can't believe there is so much sadness in me!" The sadness may spill over into his daily life; between therapy sessions, it is common for him to experience spontaneous crying during the week "for no reason." Yet the benefits of revisiting the pain are powerful. One man explained:

> Grief work is allowing me to generate my true deep sadness—feeling hurt and abandoned—all the loneliness that I wasn't able to explore as a child. I was often very sad; I felt alone in the midst of a large family, and believed that I had no right to express my true feelings of being sad when I was hurt.
>
> In grief work, I'm able to re-live that pain and experience it in a safe environment rather than bury it and deny it and fear it. I'm gradually working this through now in a healthy way. I know now that we're meant to feel the pain, not to bury it. And when I feel the pain, then my need to use the homosexuality to cover it up is so much less.

## Working Through the Abandonment – Annihilation Trauma

Essential to resolving the gender deficit of the homosexual man is the working-through of the Annihilation-Abandonment trauma that has created this core injury.

Attachment researchers, most notably John Bowlby, explain the infantile attachment process as rooted in a primal drive which, when thwarted, leaves as its legacy a sense of loss that is almost equivalent to physical death. Human attachment needs are rooted in the drive for basic survival. Therefore, the man who has suffered an attachment loss will re-experience it as something like the feeling of falling into a bottomless abyss—actually, dying.

The injury may have first begun with an insecure attachment to the mother. That hurt is profoundly re-experienced when the boy makes his first gestures toward fulfilling his masculine ambition and reaches out to the father, then finds himself unacknowledged. When rejection from other boys follows, the attachment wound deepens.

When an attachment loss is experienced, the child can neither share his distress, nor even accurately conceptualize the actual nature of his loss. Gender is intrinsic to the structure of self, in the very same manner that support beams are intrinsic to the strength of a building. And so his unmet needs will persist, and the loss will be stored within his body memory. The developmental sequence is therefore: 1) core attachment loss; 2) resulting gender-identity deficit; 3) compensation through homo-erotic reparation.

Any time this primal attachment bond fails to develop, the person must address the shame of *not having felt authentically known and validated.* When he becomes an adult, he must acknowledge and grieve this loss. Grief resolution allows him to release these body-held memories, and in the process, to mourn their loss.

As we have seen, within the Triadic-Narcissistic structure, the boy's attempts at individualization and gender actualization were not adequately supported within the family. The results will be disastrous for the gentle and temperamentally sensitive boy, whose male peers will be quick to reinforce the message that he is, indeed, somehow weak, inferior, and defective.

The pre-homosexual boy experiences this attachment rupture differently with each parent. He commonly reports that he felt ignored/criticized by his father, and manipulated/emotionally over-engaged by his mother. *Both parents may indeed have loved the child within the limitations of their own personalities.* However, their interactions communicated to the sensitive child, on some level, that who he really was, was somehow not acceptable.

## Learning to Live Authentically

The literature on the psychology of bereavement reveals the legacy of unfinished grieving in any person's life: particularly, a pathological fear of emotional closeness, and a constrained capacity for genuine intimacy. This defensive avoidance of authentic emotions, which serves to protect against the core narcissistic hurt, is seen in the Shame Posture (formerly called Defensive Detachment), which we so characteristically observe in the men who come to us with same-sex attractions.

Understandably, the therapist will encounter significant resistance against approaching this unresolved loss. Seeing his client struggle through this death-like experience may bring up the therapist's own discomfort with grief, and perhaps require that he face his own unresolved losses. Further, he must be willing to return with some clients again and again—as necessary—to this same place of profound pain. Consequently, Grief Work should never be entered into until there is sufficient positive transference to counter the entrenched defenses of both therapist and client.

Yet when we pursue this painful work in Reparative Therapy, we see profound, durable treatment gains. The more the client is able to penetrate and resolve his attachment loss, the less he will feel driven toward homosexual behavior as a form of reparation. The process proceeds as follows:

**Task #1:** To accept the reality of the loss–to come face-to-face with it.

**Task #2:** To acknowledge its meaning, to confront its significance, to *feel the emotional impact* of the loss with the support of an empathic "significant other" (in this case, an attuned therapist).

**Task #3:** To admit to oneself its irreversibility, and to accept the reality that there is no going back and undoing the experience.

## Healthy *vs* Pathological Grief

The term Grief Work was first coined by Freud. From his earliest writings, Freud understood this process to involve helping the client abandon his defenses in order to face a deep loss. He said Grief Work must involve "de-cathecting the libido" from the mental representation of the lost attachment, and when this was successfully accomplished, libido would then be reclaimed through re-cathexis into subsequent, healthy attachments.

Freud noted that success can be blocked, however, by the continuance of conflicting feelings toward the loved one; *i.e.*, when unresolved anger remains, which is then turned back against the self.

Freud's earliest formulations regarding grief remain central to our work, in that we understand homosexuality and its associated symptoms to represent a defense against an attachment loss incurred in childhood, often within the Triadic-Narcissistic family.

Grief is a natural human state which should have both a beginning, and also an end. Yet there is much personal variability in this emotional process; no two people grieve in the same way. Some people remain trapped in an intense and prolonged reaction against the loss of an emotionally important figure. Others, however, feel little need to repeatedly reenter the loss.

But until the grief is resolved, all emotional roads will lead the man back to the original Annihilation-Abandonment trauma. Perhaps of greatest concern, unfinished grieving results in a lifestyle of narcissistic self-protection.

Healthy grieving is a fully felt and conscious experience that does not involve prolonged suffering. Pathological grief, however, is marked by self-defeating, self-destructive, maladaptive behaviors.

Not surprisingly, the person with a homosexual problem often carries traits characteristic of persons stuck in pathological grief:

excessive dependency upon others for self-esteem, subclinical depression, maladaptive behaviors, suicidal ideation, emotional instability, as well as difficulty with long-term intimate relationships.

We have observed all of those symptoms to exist at a high rate of frequency among our homosexually oriented clients. In fact, a much higher-than-average rate of psychiatric disorders has been shown, in recent studies, to exist among all homosexual men—not just within clinical populations, and not just in cultures that are hostile to gay relationships, but in gay-tolerant societies as well.[1]

In fact, the variety of the maladaptive behaviors of gay men is so broad that it argues persuasively for the existence of an early, profound injury.

When unresolved grief is a ground-source of same-sex desires, we can understand why we would observe so many self-defeating, maladaptive behaviors among gay men. Homoeroticism serves to mask the anguish of this profound loss and functions as a temporary, if ultimately unsatisfying, distraction from the fundamental loss of a core attachment injury.

One might say it is ironic that "gay" is the word used to describe a defense against profound sadness; because homosexual acting-out, for such men, is a narcissistic defense against truly mourning the lack of an authentic attachment to one or both parents. The homosexual condition can, for these men, be understood as a symptom of chronic and pathological grief.

Whenever we as therapists return the client to his unfinished bereavement, he will be increasingly freed from the grief and shame that have been paralyzing his assertion and propelling him into a life unnaturally constrained within the straitjacket of the False Self.

---

## Reference

[1] *See*, for example, Sandfort, T.G., de Graaf, R., Bijl, R.V, Schnabel, P. (2001), "Same-Sex Sexual Behavior and Psychiatric Disorders: Findings from the Netherlands Mental Health Survey and Incidence Study (NEMESIS)," *Archives of General Psychiatry* 58: 85-91.

## Chapter Eighteen

# The Masculine Type of Homosexual Man

I am often asked, "If homosexuality is usually caused by an internalized sense of masculine inferiority, how do you explain the masculine type of homosexual?"

I explain it as follows. In most such cases, the reparative principle is the same: there is an eroticized attempt to capture the lost masculine self. We see the same internal sense of masculine deficit that we see in the androgynous or feminine type of homosexual man. But in boyhood, this man needed to develop an external "macho" personality to fend off emotional abuse. For example, the very masculine actor, Rock Hudson, the quintessential "heart throb" of the 1960's, confessed: "There is a little girl inside of me" (Davidson, 1986).

An early environment of severe humiliation has taught some men not to show weakness, and to have contempt for their own vulnerability. The bullying they experienced typically came from the father, an older brother, or male peers at school. To show weakness often provoked greater assault, and so denial of their vulnerability was necessary for survival.

The maneuver into a hyper-masculine façade is a "reaction formation," which entails, as Freud said, an "identification with the aggressor." It is a primitive form of self-protection in which the victim gains a fantasy security by imitating the feared person.[1]

This same shift in identity is also seen in the masculine lesbian who in many cases, perceived her mother—and therefore femininity—as weak and characterized by victimhood; to defend herself from falling into a similar position, the daughter joins up, through identification, with the father, and she becomes "Daddy's little 'boy.'"

## Giving Love to a Child as a Form of Sexual "Reparation"

The masculine-type homosexual man will usually displace his own need for love, comfort and protection onto a younger, weaker male. This is similar to the situation we see in another sexual deviation, pedophilia, where the adult wishes to "give love" to a boy because he himself felt unloved and unprotected in his childhood. The "innocent young boy" image the pedophile is so drawn to, is a projection of the abandoned little boy that still exists within himself.

Self-psychology explains this scenario—a person's displacement of his own unmet needs onto his "disavowed" self, now envisioned in the image of another person—as a form of narcissistic identification. When this masculine type of homosexual man feels

insecure, he resorts to the reparative sexual enactment of giving comfort to the frightened boy within, by seeking closeness with a vulnerable younger man. Therefore, he is often attracted to the innocent, adolescent type of partner who represents the suppressed part of himself that had to be denied in order for him to survive his boyhood. So he gives protection and "love" (albeit contaminated by sexuality) to the youth, a protection which he himself once longed for but never found.

Therapy necessitates guiding the client toward abandoning his false, hyper-masculine facade and discovering a genuine, healthy masculine self. A genuine masculine self is characterized by, among other things, an emotional openness, along with attendant vulnerability.

The process also requires resolving his childhood trauma of abuse and intimidation. When these traumas are recognized, revisited, and then resolved, the client gradually abandons his compulsion to enact a reparative search for the "vulnerable little boy within" in another man.

---

**End Note:**

[1] This phenomenon is similar to the Stockholm Syndrome, in which captives come to identify with their abductors. The case of Patty Hearst, heiress to the Hearst media empire, is an intriguing example. For two months, Patty was kept in a closet and "brainwashed" by her captors, culminating with her assimilating into their identity. As a willing convert to their revolution, she then took the name "Tanya" (a tribute to the wife of Che Guevara) and participated in the robbery of a San Francisco bank.

---

**Reference:**

Davidson, Sara (1986), *Rock Hudson: His Story.* New York: Morrow.

## Chapter Nineteen

# Fathers of Homosexuals

*We cannot ignore the striking commonality of these fathers' personalities.*

It is widely agreed that many factors contribute to the formation of male homosexuality, and that one common factor is the biological influence of a sensitive temperament (Byne and Parsons, 1993). No scientific evidence, however, shows homosexuality itself to be directly inherited, in the sense that eye color is inherited (Satinover, 1996).

Political pressure has resulted in the suppression of the older clinical evidence—which strongly implicates *developmental factors, particularly the influence of parents,* in homosexual development.

A review of the literature on male homosexuality reveals extensive reference to the pre-homosexual boy's relational problems with both parents (West 1959, Socarides 1978, Evans 1969). Among many researchers, the father-son relationship has been particularly implicated as pivotal (Bieber *et al.,* 1962, Moberly 1983).

One strongly supported hypothesis for the connection between a poor father-son relationship and homosexuality is that during the critical gender-identity phase of development, the boy perceives the father as disinterested or rejecting. As a result, he grows up failing to fully identify with his father and the masculinity he represents.

The likely cause for the boy's "failure to identify" is a narcissistic injury inflicted by the father onto the son (a son who is temperamentally sensitive) during the toddler stage of the boy's development. This is the phase when the boy must undertake the task of assuming a masculine identification. The injury in relationship to the father manifests itself as a defensive detachment from the father and what he represents—*i.e.*, masculinity.

It means the boy will reject as "*not me*" the developing masculinity he senses in himself. In adulthood, he will seek that masculinity in other men. Because it was not fully internalized within himself, masculinity remains an alien and mysterious quality. We often see, in homosexual men, a lifelong complex of "the hurt little boy" (Nicolosi, 1991) who never quite grows up.

During the course of my treatment of ego-dystonic homosexual men, I have sometimes requested that fathers participate in their son's treatment. Thus I have been able to familiarize myself with some of the fathers' most common personality traits. This discussion attempts to identify some clinical features common to them.

For this report, I have focused on sixteen fathers whom I consider typical in my practice—twelve fathers of homosexual sons (mid-teens to early 30's), and four fathers of young, gender-disturbed, evidently pre-homosexual boys (4- to 7- year-olds).

The vast majority of these fathers appeared to be psychologically normal and (also, like most fathers) well-intentioned with regard to their sons; in only one case was the father seriously disturbed, inflicting significant emotional cruelty. However, as a group, these men were characterized by an inability to counter the defensive detachment that their sons had developed in relation to them. They felt helpless to attract the boy into their own masculine sphere.

## Clinical Impressions

These men were typically, emotionally avoidant. Exploration of their histories revealed that they usually had suffered from poor relationships with their own fathers. They tended to defer to their wives in emotional matters and appeared particularly dependent on them to be their guides, interpreters and spokespersons. (For a classic example of this scenario, see the biography of actor Montgomery Clift, described here in Chapter 15)

While these men expressed sincere hope that their sons would transition to heterosexuality, nevertheless they proved incapable of living up to a long-term commitment to help them toward that goal. In his first conjoint session, for example, one father cried openly as his 15-year-old son expressed his deep disappointment with him; yet for months afterward, he would take the boy to his appointment without saying a word to him during the drive there in the car.

Further, while they often appeared to be gregarious and popular, these fathers tended not to have significant male friendships. The extent to which they lacked the ability for male emotional encounter was too consistent and pronounced to be dismissed as simply "typical of the American male." Rather, my impression of these men as a group was that there existed some significant limitation in their ability to engage emotionally with males.

From their sons' earliest years, these fathers showed considerable variation in their ability to recognize and respond to the boys' emotional withdrawal from them. Some naively reported their perception of having had a "great" relationship with their sons, while their sons themselves described the relationship as having been "terrible." Approximately half the fathers, however, sadly admitted that the relationship was always poor and, in retrospect, perceived their sons as *rejecting them* from early childhood.

*Why* their sons rejected them remained for most fathers a mystery, and they could only express a helpless sense of resignation and confusion.

When pushed, these men would go further to express hurt and deep sadness. Ironically, these same sentiments—helplessness, hurt and confusion—seemed to be mutually experienced by their sons: they are the same sentiments expressed by almost all my clients in describing their own feelings about their fathers.

The overarching trait common to fathers seemed to be an incapacity to summon the ability to correct relational problems.

All the men reported feeling "stuck" and helpless in the face of their sons' indifference or explicit rejection. Rather than actively extending themselves, they were characteristically inclined to retreat, avoid, and stay stuck in their own sense of hurt. Preoccupied with self-protection and unwilling to risk the vulnerability required to give of themselves in a relationship, they were unable to close the emotional breach. Some showed narcissistic personality features that limited their empathy. Some of them were harsh and capable of severe criticism; others were brittle and rigid; but most were soft, weak and placid, with a characteristic emotional inadequacy. The term that comes to mind for all of them is the classic psychoanalytic term "acquiescent"—the acquiescent father. They simply gave up and withdrew from the relationship as a result of their perplexity.

Homosexuality is almost certainly due to multiple factors and cannot be reduced solely to a faulty father-son relationship. We know that fathers of homosexual sons are usually fathers of heterosexual sons too, so the personality of the father is clearly not the sole cause of homosexuality.

The other contributing factors I have seen in my practice are a hostile, feared older brother; a mother who is a very warm and attractive personality and proves more appealing to the boy than an emotionally removed father; a mother who is actively disdainful of masculinity; childhood seduction by another male; and peer labelling and cruelty due to the boy's clumsiness, timidity, or obesity. Sometimes there was a physical deformity that caused them to be teased relentlessly; in another case, there was congenital deafness. All of these factors resulted in the boys' exclusion from the world of males and caused them to grow up feeling like outsiders. We usually also see a particularly sensitive, relatively fragile, often passive disposition which makes it hard for such a boy to fight back.

In recent years, there have also been strong cultural factors encouraging a confused and uncertain youngster into the gay community.

In two cases I dealt with, the fathers were very involved and deeply committed to the treatment of their sons, but conceded that they were not emotionally present during their sons' early years. In those cases, it was not personality, but circumstance that caused the fathers' distance. In one situation the father was a surgeon who reported having attended medical school and being essentially a stranger to his children while trying to provide financial support for them.

The second father I am thinking of, an auto mechanic from the Midwest, reported that when he was just 21 years old, he was forced to marry the boy's mother because she was pregnant. He admitted never loving the boy's mother, having been physically absent from the home, and essentially having abandoned both mother and boy.

Both of the above-mentioned fathers, in later life more mature and committed to re-establishing contact with their sons, participated enthusiastically in their therapy. But it was too late. Their sons had, by then, become resistant to establishing an emotional connection.

## Attempts at Therapeutic Dialogue

My impression of fathers in conjoint sessions was almost always of a sense of helplessness, discomfort and awkwardness when required to directly interact with their sons. They tended not to trust psychological concepts and communication techniques and often seemed confused and overwhelmed with the challenge to dialogue in depth. Instructions which I offered during consultation, when followed, were followed literally, mechanically and without spontaneity. A mutual antipathy, a stubborn resistance, and a deep grievance on the part of both fathers and sons was clearly observable.

At times I felt myself being placed in the too-familiar (within these families) position of having to be "mother interpreter"—a role encouraged for me by fathers and at times even by sons. As "mother interpreter," I found myself having to infer feeling and intent from the father's fragmented phrases. I was expected to convey that fuller meaning to the son, and vice versa from son to father.

Some fathers expressed concern with "saying the wrong thing," while others seemed paralyzed by fear. During dialogue, they demonstrated great difficulty in getting past their own self-consciousness and their own reactions to what their sons were saying. This limited their empathetic attunement. They had trouble grasping their son's position and his (typically, more readily expressed) feelings.

As the sons spoke to them, these fathers seemed blocked and unable to respond. Often they could only respond by saying that they were "too confused," "too hurt," or "too frustrated" to dialogue. One father said he was "too angry" to attend the sessions of his teenage son—a message conveyed to me by the mother. And at the slightest sign of improvement in the father-son relationship, some fathers seemed too ready to flee therapy, concluding "Everything is okay—can I go now?"

## Treatment Interventions

Before conjoint father-son sessions begin, the client should be helped to gain a clear sense of what he wants from his father. To simply expose him to a list of complaints is of no value. He should also decide on a clear, constructive way to ask for what he wants. Such preparation shifts the son from a position of helpless complaining, to staying centered on his genuine needs and on their effective expression.

## The Deadly Dilemma

Eventually, within the course of sessions a particular point will be reached which I call "the deadly dilemma." This deadlock in dialogue—which seems to duplicate the earliest father-son rupture—occurs in two phases as follows:

**Phase 1**: With the therapist's assistance, the son expresses his needs and wants to his father. Hearing him, the father becomes emotionally affected, so much so that he cannot respond to his son's disclosure. He is overwhelmed by his own internal reactions, becoming so "angered," "hurt," "upset," or "confused" that he cannot attend to his son's needs. Thus blocked, he is unable to give what his son asks of him.

**Phase 2**: In turn, the son is unable to tolerate his father's insular emotional reaction in place of the affirmative and open response that he now seeks from him. To accept his father's non-responses, the son feels he must abandon the needs he has expressed to him. His only recourse is to retreat again to the defensive distancing which is already at the core of the father-son relationship. He cannot empathize with his father's non-responsiveness because to do so is painfully reminiscent of childhood patterns that are associated with his own deep hurt and anger: namely, the imperative, "My father's needs must always come before mine." The son's hurt and anger is in reaction to what appears to him to be "just more of those lame excuses" for Dad's inability to give the attention, affection or approval he has so long desired from him. Indeed, to him, this just seems like Dad's old ploy, with all the associated historical pain.

This deadly dilemma originated, I believe, during the preverbal level of infancy. As one father's recollections confirmed, "My son would never look at me. I would hold his face with my hands and force him to look at me, but he would always avert his eyes." Other men have described an "unnatural indifference" from the boy during his growing-up years.

During the course of therapy with fathers, I began to see the deep hurt in *them*—a hurt that came from their sons' indifference to their attempts (however meager) to improve the relationship.

Reflecting on his now-elderly dad, one client sadly recalled:

> *I feel sorry for my father. He always had a certain insensitivity, an emotional incompetence. Many of the interactions at home simply went over his head. He was dense, inadequate. I feel a pity for him.*

These men appeared unwilling or unable to be open and vulnerable to their sons; unable to reach out, to hear their sons' pain and anger with respect to them, and unable to respond honestly. Their emotional availability was blocked, and they simply could not turn the relational problem around. Rather they remained removed, seemingly dispassionate, and helpless.

During our sessions, none of the fathers was capable of taking the lead in dialogue. When dialogue became stagnant, they were unable to initiate communication.

We cannot ignore the striking commonality of these fathers' personalities. I believe their consistent inability to get past their own blocks and *reach out* to their sons had played a pivotal role during early family life in preventing their sons from moving forward into a full masculine identification and normal heterosexual development.

---

## References

Bieber, I. *et al* (1962) *Homosexuality: a Psychoanalytic Study of Male Homosexuals*. New York: Basic Books.

Byne, W. and Parsons, B. (1993), "Human sexual orientation: the biologic theories reappraised," *Archives of General Psychiatry* 50, pp. 228-39.

Evans, R. (1969), "Childhood parental relationships of homosexual men," *Journal of Consulting and Clinical Psychology* 33, pp.129-35.

Green, Richard (1987), *The "Sissy Boy Syndrome" and the Development of Homosexuality*, New Haven: Yale U. Press.

Moberly, Elizabeth (1983), *Homosexuality: A New Christian Ethic*, Greenwood: Attic Press.

Nicolosi, Joseph (1991, 2020), *Reparative Therapy of Male Homosexuality: a New Clinical Approach*. Northvale: Jason Aronson; Tarzana: Liberal Mind Publishers.

Satinover, J. (1996), *Homosexuality and the Politics of Truth*. Grand Rapids: Baker Books.

Socarides, Charles (1978), *Homosexuality.* New York: Jason Aronson.

West, D.J. (1959), Parental figures in the genesis of male homosexuality. *International Journal of Social Psychiatry* 5, pp. 85-97.

Zucker, K. and Bradley, S. (1995), *Gender Identity Disorder and Psychosexual Problems in Children and Adolescents.* N.Y.: The Guilford Press.

Zuger, B. (l988), "Is Early Effeminate Behavior in Boys Early Homosexuality?" *Comprehensive Psychiatry*, vol. 29, no. 5 (September/October) p. 509-19.

## Chapter Twenty

# The Power of Therapeutic Attunement

When the client opens up his emotional life to the therapist, he has engaged in an act of trust which links himself and the therapist in an intimate "dance." The central healing process of psychotherapy is the full experience of this elegant dance of attunement.

One very important lesson the client learns is the vital art of simultaneous *feeling-describing.* Typically, he has "disowned" aspects of his interior emotional life. Therefore, making that connection between *feeling* and *describing* in the presence of another person is almost always distressing to him.

When parents have failed to accurately mirror the child's internal experience and failed to model the lesson that *simultaneously feeling and expressing his feelings is safe*, the child will grow up to be emotionally disorganized and isolated. He learns to distrust his interior perceptions, and becomes prone to shame-infused shutdowns of spontaneous emotionality.

The child's defenses will cause him to shift his attention back and forth from content to feelings, and then back again to content, while avoiding making the link between the two.

At critical moments of strong emotion, I often need to encourage the client with these words: "Try to stay in contact with me and with your feelings at the same time." Establishing this neural link between *thinking* and *feeling* initiates the vital process of unification between left-brain and right-brain hemispheres, between cognitive and affective, between conscious and unconscious, through the medium of human interaction.

## Reconnecting After a Breach

Misunderstandings, hurt feelings and hidden resentments are inevitable in the therapeutic relationship. They offer the client an opportunity to learn how to reengage emotionally after a relational breach. Negotiating his way through such an experience shows the client how relationships can survive the critical process of "*attunement—misattunement—reattunement*," and reveals how relational trust, when lost, can in fact be regained.

Reattunement moments link the client back to the therapist, and also back to himself. Through this process, he gradually increases his capacity to tolerate distress in human relationships. At its best, this emotional reconnection is reminiscent of the earliest, most primal attunement between mother and child.

One can never actually "undo" a trauma of the past, of course. Yet a good therapeutic relationship can lay down new, positive neurological pathways on top of the old, traumatic experiences. For too long, these traumas have prevented the client from engaging other people through the *full sense of personhood* that he now longs to claim as his own.

## Chapter Twenty-One

# Overcoming Gay Porn

The easy availability of pornography and consequent addiction to it, has reached epidemic proportions that the media continues to ignore. For the man with same-sex attraction (SSA), gay porn becomes a particular problem because of the natural but frustrated deeper emotional desires that such porn reenacts.

It became apparent to many of my clients, as I worked with them, that porn's appeal lay in its seeming promise to satisfy three emotional drives: (1) body envy, (2) desire to develop an assertive attitude, and (3) need to experience vulnerable sharing with men.

If, upon reflection, the client agrees that his attraction to porn is rooted in the above motivations, then we proceed to work on them. If not, then we approach the issue from another direction.

Let us review each of these emotional needs described above, and see how they are represented in gay porn.

**Body Envy:** Usually the first identified need is the desire for a body like the personified image. The porn actor possesses qualities of masculinity which the client feels he lacks. For each man, those desired masculine features may differ, but the common elements are muscularity, body hair, large build, and the archetypal representation of masculinity—a large penis, which the client often feels is shamefully lacking in himself.

**Assertion:** In addition to body image, the client is drawn to a display of directness, confidence, lack of inhibition, and bold aggression. These are exactly what most clients feel they lack in their own personalities.

**Vulnerable Sharing:** With further exploration, the client may identify his attraction to porn as a desire to experience the sensation of open sharing with another man. Erotic activity between two men offers a fantasy image of such sharing, with the illusion that there is a deep level of mutual acceptance and validation. This mutuality is painfully absent in his male relationships, which are typically uncomfortable and guarded.

## Fantasy for Reality

Interest in gay porn diminishes as the client begins to understand that on a deeper level, he is pursuing normal, healthy and valid needs through his fantasy. Yet, while he is apparently emotionally "safe" with porn because he is protected from being truly known, the experience offers nothing but temporary relief from his loneliness and alienation from other men. The client is encouraged by his therapist to surrender this false form of intimacy for authentic friendship. While porn offers him momentary "safety" from the anticipation of shame-invoking rejection, it satisfies only in the moment.

The three therapeutic techniques for uncovering the client's unconscious needs are: (1) Inquiry-Investigation, (2) Body Work, and (3) EMDR (Eye-Movement Desensitization and Reprocessing). The effectiveness of each technique depends upon the client. The therapist may combine them, but as a general rule, Body Work is more effective than Inquiry-Investigation, and EMDR is more effective than Body Work. (Body Work involves the development of self-attunement, and does not involve touching.)

The client's recognition of porn as being in reality a fantasy projection of unmet needs, inevitably leads the motivated client to ask: "Well, then how *do* I get these needs met?" His question marks the second phase of Reparative Therapy and the process of coming out of porn, and more importantly, out of homosexuality itself. Preoccupation with such porn always represents the client's own sense of masculine inferiority made manifest in these three aspects, and investigation into the life of the SSA client typically reveals a deficit in authentic male friendships.

Memories of boyhood shaming by dominant males often surface during therapeutic exploration. Porn actors, after all, represent the kind of men who excite and intimidate our client. The client comes to realize that through this erotic reenactment, he can dominate (or be dominated by) the men who once frightened him. Through this reenactment he can engage in a pseudo-control of the kinds of men who have humiliated and rejected him. He "gains power" to control and humiliate men through, as one client said, "making another man melt."

As the client comes to identify how he projects onto the erotic image his unmet needs, and as he fulfills those needs in real male friendships, the compelling power of the image diminishes. Clinical reports tell us that the client may later find such erotic images not only uninteresting and non-arousing, but repellant and degrading to masculine dignity in the same way that such images are experienced by heterosexual men.

## Chapter Twenty-Two

# Why Gays Cannot Speak for Ex-Gays

A British television network once called to interview me for a show about men who sought to reduce their unwanted attractions. The host of the show, they informed me, was a gay man. I declined the invitation, stating that the host's gay identity would disqualify him from a fair evaluation of the ex-gay experience.

To refuse participation because the host is gay may seem unreasonable, until we recognize that the adoption of such an identity typically prevents someone from honestly assessing the experience of the other man who has taken a different developmental route—*i.e.,* the homosexually oriented person who chooses not to identify with his same-sex attractions.

Why would this be true? Let me explain. According to the literature, the "coming out of the closet" process begins in early adolescence with the discovery of same-sex attraction. The teenager then usually rejects his homosexual feelings because of the negative social values around him. His painful and lonely efforts to suppress, repress and deny his feelings result in guilt and shame, which eventually culminates in self-loathing.

But shortly thereafter, this teenager discovers that there are others like him, and often through the support and encouragement of a gay counselor, coach, teacher or religious leader, he decides that gay is "who he is." The adoption of this gay identity necessitates the abandonment of any hope that he could ever modify his unwanted feelings and develop his heterosexual potential. He must surrender his earlier wish that he could have a conventional marriage and family. So in order to internalize this new identity he must mourn the impossibility of ever resolving his unwanted homosexuality; *i.e.,* he must grieve the loss of what he yearned for.

It is this process of grieving his own hopes and mourning his own dreams which prevents the person who later identifies as gay from believing that change is possible for others: "If I myself could not change, how could they?" Perhaps on a deeper level, this thought is also rooted in anger: "If I cannot have what I wanted for my own life, neither should they."

Explaining this inherent bias of the gay-identified person against the ex-gay person's experience, an Orthodox Jewish friend of mine commented: "It would be like a group of rabbis deciding that they themselves would determine if Jesus really was God." "Worse," I responded. "It would be more like a person desperately trying to find God in his life, abandoning the hope and adopting atheism, then setting himself up as the person who determines the reality of God in the lives of others."

And it is that grieving process, that painful letting-go of one's dreams, that has biased the gay person's evaluation of the ex-gay experience.

However, public-policy decisions on homosexual issues are, in fact, typically determined by gay activists who carry the intrinsic prejudice described above. Because it is gay teachers who determine policy for homosexual students; gay librarians who determine what books about SSA are permitted on the library shelves; and gay mental-health professionals who get to tell the world whether any sort of sexual-orientation modification is possible.

For example, anyone who has a comment or question about APA (American Psychological Association) policy on homosexuality is referred to the Office of Lesbian, Gay, Bisexual and Transgender Concerns, which does not recognize ex-gays or the concerns of people struggling to change.

## APA Excludes Any Form of Intellectual Diversity

Worse, the most grievous and damaging example of this prejudice is the 2009 APA Task Force Report on the treatment of homosexuality,[1] written by a panel that consisted entirely of gay-activist mental-health practitioners—all of whom admitted, at the start, to being opposed to any form of reorientation therapy. No therapists who actually *practiced* reorientation therapy were included. Several applied to join the Task Force—including distinguished and prominent, peer-review-published psychologists who worked as clinicians and taught at the university level—and none was permitted to join the committee. The deck was thus stacked from the start.

This dominance of gay-identified homosexuals on panels that determine policy for all homosexuals is due, in large part, to intellectual intimidation. Subsequently, there is an avoidance of the whole polarizing issue by non-gay professionals who fear the career-killing charge of being called anti-gay.

Faced with policy decisions, the straight person, ignorant of the fact that gay-identified homosexuals are a category that is quite distinct from non-gay homosexuals, readily relinquishes his authority to his gay co-worker, and takes the easy way out. "I don't know about such things myself, of course; but Steven is gay—he'll know the best policy for the library collection." (Needless to stay, Steven is all too ready to comply, and to take control of all future book purchases in the LGBT collection.)

The sad fact, then, is that *ex*-gays become marginalized and intimidated into silence. Gay activists see these people as illegitimate; they are merely "gays-in-process," or gays with a small "g" and not entitled to claim a valid identity in their own right. Such men are seen as merely gays who have not yet come out of the closet; they require, it is said, a good dose of enlightenment, being "inhibited by their homophobia."

But the emergence of the ex-gay person into social recognition can change this balance of power. Despite the intimidating influence of pro-gay activism, society can also recognize the ex-gay person's existence, as ex-gay men and women come forward and tell us about their lives, the influences that shaped their sexuality, and their dissatisfaction with living a gay lifestyle.

Every social movement has used as a tool toward its success, the shaming and intimidating of others who do not agree with them. Those who disagree with gay activists are stigmatized and excluded from the cultural discourse. As time goes by, I believe this swing toward extremism will ultimately correct itself.

But in the meanwhile, we must look to that committed core of individuals who understand that our bodies tell us *who we are*—that humanity was designed and created for heterosexuality. And we must support those men and women who are brave enough to speak out and say, "Gay life didn't work for us; and we have changed."

---

**End Note:**

1] *Report of the APA Task Force on the Appropriate Therapeutic Responses to Sexual Orientation* (2009), <https://www.apa.org/pi/lgbt/resources/therapeutic-response.pdf>

## Chapter Twenty-Three

# An Open Secret: The Truth About Gay Male Couples

> *"Being queer means pushing the parameters of sex and family, and in the process, transforming the very fabric of society."*
>
> *—National Gay and Lesbian Task Force Policy director, Paul Ettelbrick (Kurtz, 2003)*

The promiscuous nature of homosexual relationships is recognized in the gay community as a simple fact of life. "Sexual promiscuity is one of the most striking, distinguishing features of gay life in America" says one gay-activist observer. (Hoffman, p. 45)

In 1948, Kinsey observed that long-term homosexual relationships were notably few. Now, more than seventy years later, long-term gay male relationships are more common, but a qualifying fact remains: they are typically not monogamous.

In one study of gay male couples, 41.3% had open sexual agreements with some conditions or restrictions, and 10% had open sexual agreements with no restrictions on sex with outside partners. One-fifth of participants (21.9%) reported breaking their agreement

in the preceding 12 months, and 13.2% of the sample reported having unprotected anal intercourse in the preceding three months with an outside partner of unknown or discordant HIV-status.[1]

The gay community has long walked a thin public-relations line, presenting their relationships as equivalent to those of heterosexual married couples. But gay activists themselves, while defending gay marriage, still portray a very different cultural ethic. For example, Michelangelo Signorile describes the campaign "to fight for same-sex marriage and its benefits and then, once granted, redefine the institution completely—to demand the right to marry not as a way of adhering to society's moral codes, but rather to debunk a myth and radically alter an archaic institution." (1974, p. 3).

## Research Findings On Promiscuity

A much-cited study by Bell and Weinberg (1978), published by the Kinsey Institute, and often called the most ambitious study of homosexuality ever attempted, gathered its data before the AIDS crisis had begun. This study showed that 28 percent of homosexual males had had sexual encounters with *one thousand* or more partners. Furthermore, 79 percent said more than half of their sex partners were strangers. Only one percent of the sexually active men had had fewer than five lifetime partners.

The authors concede: "Little credence can be given to the supposition that homosexual men's 'promiscuity' has been overestimated." (82) "Almost half of the white homosexual males . . . said that they had had at least 500 different sexual partners during the course of their homosexual careers." (85)

A few years later, Pollak (1985) described sexual behavior among gays as "an average several dozen partners a year" and "some hundreds in a lifetime" with "tremendous promiscuity." (44) He said:

> The homosexual pick-up system is the product of a search for efficiency and economy in attaining the maximization of

> "yield" (in numbers of partners and orgasms) and the minimization of "cost" (waste of time and risk of one's advances being rejected). Certain places are known for a particular clientele and immediate consummation: such as "leather" bars, which often have a back room specially reserved for the purpose, saunas and public parks. (44)

William Aaron's autobiographical book *Straight* draws similar conclusions about gay life as he lived it:

> In the gay life, fidelity is almost impossible. Since part of the compulsion of homosexuality seems to be a need on the part of the homophile to "absorb" masculinity from his sexual partners, he must be constantly on the lookout for [new partners]. Consistently, the most successful homophile "marriages" are those where there is an agreement between the two to have affairs on the side while maintaining the semblance of permanence in their living arrangement. (208)

He concludes:

> Gay life is most typical and works best when sexual contacts are impersonal and even anonymous. As a group the homosexuals I have known seem far more preoccupied with sex than heterosexuals are, and far more likely to think of a good sex life as many partners under many exciting circumstances. (209)

## Emphasis On Sexuality

One writer—who, it should be mentioned, strongly sympathized with the gay community about the stresses of social discrimination—observes conditions among gay men as follows:

> It must be remembered that in the gay world the only real criterion of value is physical attractiveness . . . . The young homosexual will find that his homosexual brothers usually only care for him as a sexual object. Although they may invite him out to dinner and give him a place to stay, when they have satisfied their sexual interest in him, they will likely forget about his existence and his own personal needs . . . . Since the sole criterion of value in the homosexual world is physical attractiveness, being young and handsome in gay life is like being a millionaire in a community where wealth is the only criterion of value. (Hoffman, 1968, pp. 58, 153, 155)

Aging is also viewed particularly negatively in the homosexual culture, with high value placed on youth. (Bell and Weinberg, 1978)

In his psychoanalytic study of ten couples, six of whom were homosexual, Gershman (1981) observed that in homosexual coupling, "sexuality is of greater importance and plays a larger role." Gershman found that the majority of male couples he studied had agreed upon an open relationship, as long as the affairs were conducted discreetly. He found that while the male couples studied were capable of high compatibility in many other respects, there was great difficulty in maintaining sexual interest.

With the exception of the pioneering work of Warren (1974), for many years, little attention was given to long term gay relationships. When McWhirter and Mattison published *The Male Couple* in 1984, their study was undertaken to disprove the reputation that gay male relationships do not last. The authors themselves were a homosexual couple, one a psychiatrist, the other a psychologist. After much searching they were able to locate 156 male couples in relationships that had lasted from 1 to 37 years. Two-thirds of the respondents had entered the relationship with either the implicit or the explicit expectation of sexual fidelity.

The results of their study show that of those 156 couples, only seven had been able to maintain sexual fidelity. Furthermore, of those seven couples, none had been together more than five years. In other words, *the researchers were unable to find a single male couple that was able to maintain sexual fidelity for more than five years.* They reported:

> The expectation for outside sexual activity was the rule for male couples and the exception for heterosexuals. Heterosexual couples lived with some expectation that their relationships were to last "until death do us part," whereas gay couples wondered if their relationships could survive. (3)

Outside affairs, the researchers found, were not damaging to the relationship's endurance, but were in fact essential to its very *survival.* "The single most important factor that keeps couples together past the ten-year mark is the lack of possessiveness they feel," say the authors. (256)

McWhirter and Mattison admit that sexual activity outside the relationship often raises issues of distrust, damage to self-esteem, and disagreement about level of mutual dependency. However, they believe that:

> Many couples learn very early in their relationship that ownership of each other sexually can become the greatest internal threat to their staying together. (256)

Other researchers, too, have seen sexual freedom as beneficial to gay relationships. (Harry, 1978, Peplau, 1982)

Yet in reality, there remains a contradictory longing for greater stability.

In a study of thirty couples, Hooker (1965, p. 46) found that all but three couples expressed "an intense longing for relationships with stability, sexual continuity, intimacy, love and affection"—but only one couple in her study had been able to maintain a monogamous relationship for ten years. Hooker concluded, "For many homosexuals, one-night stands or short-term relationships are typical." (49)

The desire for sexual fidelity in relationships and the benefits of such a commitment are universal. *In the long history of man, infidelity has never been associated with maturity.* Even in cultures where it is relatively common, it is no more than discreetly tolerated.

Faced with the fact that gay male relationships are in fact promiscuous, gay writers have no choice but to promote the counter-intuitive message that monogamy is neither necessary nor desirable.

McWhirter and Mattison believe that gays must redefine "fidelity" to mean not sexual faithfulness, but simply "emotional dependability."

But how can a relationship without sexual fidelity remain emotionally faithful? Fidelity as such is only an abstraction, divorced from the body. The agreement to have outside affairs precludes any possibility of genuine trust and intimacy.

## A Clinical Understanding of Gay Infidelity: Being Unfree to Fully Love

Gay relationships are typically burdened with each man's same-sex defensive detachment, and their need to compensate for that detachment. Therefore, the relationship will often take the form of an unrealistic idealization of the other person as an "image" of an ideal man. In pursuing the other man as a representation of the masculine introject that he himself lacks, many gay men either develop a self-denigrating dependency on the partner, or they become disillusioned because they soon discover "he has the same masculine deficit I have."

As he did in relationship with his father, the homosexual man fails to fully and accurately perceive the other person. His same-sex ambivalence and defensive detachment mitigate against the development of trust and intimacy. When he becomes disillusioned with his partner, he will continually set his hopes on the possibility of yet another, more satisfying partner, if he can only find him.

In seeking out and sexualizing relationships with other males, the homosexual is attempting to integrate a lost part of himself. Because this attraction emerges out of a deficit, he is not completely free to love. He perceives other men in terms of what they can do to make him feel better about himself. Thus, a giving of the self may seem more like a diminishment, than a fulfillment.

A man who is depressed will gain a temporary sense of mastery through anonymous sex because of its excitement, intensity, even danger—followed by sexual release and an immediate reduction of tension and depression. Later he is likely to feel disgusted, remorseful, and out of control. He feels regretful, regains control, and then feels all right again. But when there is nothing in his life to "feed" that healthy state, it will be a matter of time until he gets depressed, feels powerless and out of touch with himself, and seeks anonymous sex again as a short-term solution to getting back in touch and feeling in control.

Often a homosexual client will report seeking anonymous sex following an incident in which he felt ignored or slighted by another male. Feeling shamed and victimized, he acts out sexually as a way of reasserting himself and getting something back he feels was taken from him. Once again, he feels guilty and has to repent or make amends. Many gay men become addicted not just to the sexual release, but to the entire compulsive, life-dominating cycle—if not through overt behavior, then through preoccupation and fantasy.

In these repetitive, compulsive, and impersonal sexual behaviors, we see a focused engagement with the object—with a desire for an intense relationship, but at the same time, a resistance toward genuine intimacy. Hoffman (1968) describes the "sex fetishization" found in gay life (168), and Gottlieb (1977) points out the strong element of sexual fantasy that has become institutionalized in gay culture. Masters and Johnson (1979) also found that those fantasies tend to be more violent than those of heterosexuals.

Homosexual attraction is often characterized by a localized response to body parts or aspects of the person, but when interest in these traits diminishes through familiarity, there follows a loss of interest in the person as a whole. In comparison, "straight" men are generally, in my clinical experience, not as trait-fixated. While some men may envision their ideal woman as tall, blond, blue-eyed, and large-breasted, we hardly see a distinct disinterest in women without these specific traits.

## The Problem of Sexual Sameness

In homosexual sex, the "body parts don't fit." Therefore, sex must be "individually enjoyed rather than mutually experienced" (214) by a technique of "my turn – your turn" (214) and "you do me, I do you." (Masters and Johnson, 1979) Where orgasmic episodes are experienced separately, considerable discussion is required for their negotiation.

Sexual sameness also diminishes long-term interest and creates the need for greater variety, including other partners (Masters and Johnson 1979).

McWhirter and Mattison (1984) corroborate this viewpoint, saying, "The equality and similarities found in male couples are formidable obstacles to continuing high sexual vitality in their lasting relationships." (134)

Thus, the similarities between two men provide one possible explanation for gay promiscuity. Women are "wired" for nurturance and child-rearing, and a stable primary relationship with a protector is necessary for both mother and children to thrive. Thus a woman introduces a restraining influence into the relationship that two men, with their sameness, will never experience together.

Indeed, gay-activist social commentator Andrew Sullivan has found that as a gay man matures, his relationships will likely split between those men he is friends with, and those he has sex with, but that the two groups will not likely overlap. Gay men, he says, "have a need for extramarital outlets." (1995, p. 95)

This "new order" approach advocated by gay activists is part of a general cynicism toward mainstream values and the possibility of monogamy. Churchill, for example, is a gay advocate and a strong critic of Judeo-Christian influence in society. His work in the social-science literature reveals a deep hopelessness about the possibility of enduring relationships, either homosexual or heterosexual, and an utter cynicism about marriage:

> It may be reasonably supposed that there never was nor ever will be any person who can fulfill all of the spiritual and physical needs of another person. Hence, husbands and wives alike must spend a good deal of time and effort in artful deception and flattery . . . . They must sustain the illusion upon which their marriage is based and upon which their sexual relationship is justified. (1967, p. 301)

Churchill describes the "dreary" picture brought to mind by the term *family man*:

> It is difficult . . . to imagine any person who is engaged with the world at large as a family man or a homebody. It is almost impossibility for any man or woman who is laden with the cares and preoccupations particular to family life to be very deeply concerned with others. (305)

Of the traditional Judeo-Christian family, he says:

> Far from being the source of each and every good, it is one source of a great many social and moral evils. If all the homely virtues are learned in the bosom of the family . . . it should not be forgotten that many of the more contemptible vices are also learned in the bosom of the family: complacency, jealousy, bigotry, narrow-mindedness, envy, selfishness, rivalry, avarice, prejudice, vanity, and greed. (304)

In conclusion, although homosexuals do lack some cultural supports, such as the freedom in every culture to marry a same-sex partner, I believe this is not the cause of gay promiscuity. I believe the central cause of gay promiscuity is to be found in the inherent sexual and emotional incompatibility between two males.

Men were designed for women, and when some factor—psychological, biological, or a combination of both—interferes with that wired-in design, the freedom to marry a same-sex partner cannot change this simple reality: "*something's not working*."

In fact, Dr. Robert Spitzer, architect of the 1973 decision by the American Psychiatric Association to remove homosexuality from the diagnostic manual—and a longtime champion of gay rights—used *just those same words* to describe what he believed, "intuitively," about the nature of the homosexual condition:

> So, if you had pushed me to re-examine the 1973 definition, that is what I would argue. I would say, it is still not a disorder, but . . . I intuitively think that something is not working.

When asked if he would want his own son to get therapy, Spitzer replied:

> I would hope that he would be interested in changing and if he would be, that he would get some help. If he really were not interested in changing, I would hope I would not pressure him.

Asked about the growing push from gay activists to make such therapy unethical, he said:

> I think this is absurd. It is ridiculous . . . to say that this is unethical, I think that is ridiculous. [2]

For additional data, see NARTH (2009), "Romantic Relationship Difficulties," (pp. 70-71), "Interpersonal Relationships," (pp. 80-81) and "Promiscuity as a New Social Norm," (pp. 81-3), in *Journal of Human Sexuality* 1, www.narth.com.

---

## Endnotes

[1] Neilands, Torsten B.; Chakravarty, Deepalika; Darbes, Lynae A.; Beougher, Sean C.; and Hoff, Colleen C. (2010), "Development and Validation of the Sexual Agreement Investment Scale," *Journal of Sex Research*, 47: 1, 24-37, April 2009.

[2] https://www.dijg.de/english/homosexuality-reality-of-change/

**References:**

Aaron, William, (1972), *Straight*: A *Heterosexual Talks about his Homosexual Past,* New York: Bantam Books.

Bell, A., and Weinberg, M. (1978), *Homosexualities: a Study of Diversity among Men and Women.* New York: Simon & Schuster.

Churchill, W. (1967), *Homosexual Behavior Among Males: a Cross-cultural and Cross-species Investigation.* New York: Hawthorne Books.

Gershman, H. (1981), "Homosexual Marriages," *American Journal of Psychoanalysis* 41:149-59.

Gottlieb, D. (1977), *The Gay Tapes.* Briarcliff Manor, NY: Stein and Day Scarborough House.

Harry, J. (1978), "Marriages between gay males," in *The Social Organization of Gay Males,* ed. J. Harry and V. Devall. New York: Praeger.

Hoffman, M. (1968), *The Gay World: Male Homosexuality and the Social Creation of Evil,* New York: Basic Books.

Hooker, E. (1965), "An empirical study of some relations between sexual patterns and gender identity in male homosexuals," in *Sex Research, New Developments,* ed. J. Money, pp.24-52, New York: Holt, Reinhart and Winston.

Kinsey, A.C., Pomeroy, W.B. and Martin, C.E. (1948), *Sexual Behavior in the Human Male.* Philadelphia, PA: W.B. Saunders.

Kurtz, Stanley, "Beyond gay marriage," *The Weekly Standard*, August 4 - August 11, 2003, vol. 8, No. 45.

Masters, W., and Johnson, V. (1979), *Homosexuality in Perspective*, Boston, MA: Little, Brown.

McWhirter, D., and Mattison, A. (1984), *The Male Couple: How Relationships Develop*, Englewood Cliffs, NJ: Prentice-Hall.

Peplau, L. (1982), "Research on homosexual couples: an overview. *Journal of Homosexuality* 8:3-7.

Pollak, M. (1985), "Male homosexuality," In *Western Sexuality: Practice and Precept in Past and Present Times*, ed. P. Aries and A. Bejin, pp. 40-61. New York: Basil Blackwell.

Signorile, Michaelangelo (1994), "Bridal Wave." in *Out*, December 1994.

Sullivan, Andrew (1995), *Virtually Normal: An Argument about Homosexuality*, New York: Knopf.

Warren, C. (1974), *Identity and Community in the Gay World*. New York: Wiley & Sons.

### Chapter Twenty-Four

# Grieving the Attachment Loss

*The gender-identity phase of development is marked by a surge of "ambition" to achieve gender competence. When there is a failure in this phase, a core-identity injury results.*

*Grief work helps the client overcome the injury.*

The triadic narcissistic family offers a useful model for understanding male homosexuality, and its foundation as being rooted in a failure of attachment to the same-sex parent. The narcissistic family is not found among all same-sex attracted (SSA) men; however, we do often see evidence of this family type in our clinical work.

In healthy families, children know they are important, and they sense their needs and feelings as important to their parents. But rather than providing an understanding, accurately attuned, and supportive emotional environment for the son's developing masculine self, the narcissistic parents, as a parental team, systematically "fail to see" the boy as a gendered individual person.

## Failure to Elicit the Boy's Masculinity

Research suggests (although it has not proven) that some boys may have experienced a biological developmental "accident" in which their developing brain was never completely masculinized while they were still in utero. [1] When such children reach the gender-identity phase of about two years old, the "surge of ambition" to achieve masculine competency will be much weaker than that of the typical boy. According to reparative-drive theory, such a boy will fail to develop a normal masculine gender identity if the parents do not actively elicit it from him. Such parents did not actively "shame" the son for his strivings, but simply failed to be attuned to the boy's special need for active support in calling forth his true, gendered nature.

## The Problem of Malattunement

In the narcissistic family, there is a parental malattunement. The boy thus feels unsupported in his efforts to acquire a masculine self-identity.

In such a family, the child must be "for" the parents, *i.e.*, "the parental team." The malattunement he most often experienced was through being ignored/belittled by his father, and in the case of his mother, being manipulated into taking on the role of her intimate companion and "special" son.

The boy will feel anger turned against himself, which is a defense against his weakness and inability to break away from his mother in order to acquire a distinct and separate masculine identity. In addition to that anger against the self, the child may have been made to feel bad about his feeling sad. "You're upsetting everybody else . . . there's no reason to be unhappy, and you have nothing to complain about."

Within this family structure, the boy's unsuccessful attempts at gender actualization result in an attachment loss. Together, the parents evoked an abandonment-annihilation trauma within the boy, regarding which he now, as a man, must grieve.

This is the core trauma in the context of the narcissistic family background which has led to the homosexual man's same-sex attraction in adulthood.

## The Boy's Temperament as a Factor

Temperament is a key factor in the failure to gender-identify. Another boy who was less temperamentally sensitive—perhaps even this boy's own brother who was more outgoing, emotionally resilient, physically active, and assertive—would push harder and be more persistent in seeking his father's attention, making it less easy for the father to detach from him. By the same token, this same tough, assertive and outgoing boy often has more in common with the father, and will be actively sought out by him as a companion. The assertive-resilient boy will also be less likely to form an over-intimacy with the mother and to seek out her sheltering protections as a means of avoiding the masculine challenge.

Thus, it is the emotionally vulnerable boy—sensitive, intuitive, sociable, gentle, easily hurt—who is most likely to incur a gender-identity injury and to give up the masculine challenge. He needed special help to leave the comfortable sphere of the mother; and perhaps his father did not actively injure him, but simply failed to do the essential job—the job that was essential *for this particular boy*—of actively calling forth his latent masculine nature.

## Attachment Loss and Shame

My clients express not only a sense of gender deficit, but a deeper, not easily articulated sense of loss and emptiness. Various men have tried to describe it in their own way. It is this despairing place that is the source of the homosexual impulse. It is also the source of the client's deepest resistance to treatment.

The developmental sequence is first attachment loss, then gender deficit.

Later in life, he unconsciously seeks to "repair" the deficit through homosexual enactment. Said one client:

> When I went into the gay porn sites, as soon as I got started, I realized how depressed I had been. I realized, too, that I knew I was depressed but was avoiding doing anything about it.
>
> The power of gay porn images reflects my own inadequacy. The power of the image is not what he is, but what I am not. And I can go pursue the distraction of what he is, or confront the painful reality of what I am not.

The gender-identity phase, like all other phases of the child's development, is marked by a surge of "ambition" to achieve a particular competence. Along with this biologically driven ambition comes a narcissistic investment in the outcome. When there is a failure in that phase of development, there is a vulnerability to shame. Thus, we see not just a gender-identity deficit, but also a *core identity injury,* which brings us to the use of grief work.

The person with a homosexual problem will exhibit psychological features commonly found in any client who has become "stuck" in unexpressed pathological grief. Those include excessive dependency upon others for self-esteem, emotional maladaptation and insecurity, thoughts of suicide, and difficulty in establishing and maintaining long-term intimate relationships.

These symptoms are a defense against mourning the loss of authentic attachment to both parents. Thus, it is ironic that declaring himself "gay" is the man's defense against profound, underlying sadness.

The therapist will attempt to offer a corrective experience; *i.e.*, serving as the good parent by hearing, understanding and even valuing the experience of grief. He must also recognize and interpret the client's primary defense, which is his anticipation of being shamed for allowing himself to feel his loss. *This is the essential function of shame—to defend against grief.* It is easier to blame himself (and spend the rest of life punishing himself for not having felt "seen" or loved for who he was) than to face the profound reality of loss of the parent's *accurate attunement* and the attachment he should have had with his father. The client must openly share that shame with the therapist, in order to engage the opportunity for healing.

Grief work is often met with deeply entrenched resistance, precisely because of the intense pain resulting from the loss of attachment. *The client literally feels that if he expresses his pain, he will die.* This primal feeling is biologically rooted and is seen in the behavior of animals who live in packs; after all, the shunned, rejected member of the wolf pack rightly senses that he will not be able to survive by himself, alone; he must beg his way back into acceptability.

It is not the pain, but the fear of the pain which is the greater source of resistance in grief work. The desperate quality of this distress is understandable since, from childhood, separation meant annihilation. Now, as an adult, the client in therapy is still not secure in the belief that he can enter into that terrible, deep, primal-pain experience and survive. So it is not just reliving the trauma, but the *fear* of reliving it which is the greatest source of resistance.

Grief work is approached through the client's own presenting complaints and his self-identified conflicts. Those conflicts often involve his shame for efforts at masculine assertion. The conflicts, when pursued, often lead the man into deeper emotions. Most often, sad and angry feelings will surface when the client allows himself to fully feel the despair and emptiness associated with his attachment loss.

The next phase of therapy requires a meaningful integration of the loss. As an adult now, the client can re-create a coherent narrative—namely, the making of meaning in the present, of his attachment losses from the past.

Resolution means the client must decide to live in a realistic present, making realistic plans for the future. He must choose to have a healthy perception of reality with the people in his life today—not needing them to be better than they are. No longer do we see that inarticulate sense of narcissistic entitlement that others are obliged to compensate him for his past hurts.

This grief work is a humanizing process, in that it demands the abandonment of narcissistic defenses against experiencing deep humility. The work of grief is the back-and-forth tension between two inhibiting feelings—shame and fear, versus the other two core feelings—sadness and anger.

Resolution requires the assimilation of the loss into one's personal schema—one's worldview or personal narrative. That narrative requires a coherent understanding of himself today. As the client faces his illusions and distortions, he spontaneously expresses curiosity about his true identity. "Who am I, other than my false self?"

Resolution is the catalyst for personal growth, identity transformation, and the establishment of new ways of relating. It means growing beyond emotional isolation and chronic loneliness, and making a renewed investment in authentic relatedness with people of both genders. Along with this greater capacity for genuine intimacy, comes a welcome diminishment of same-sex attraction's illusionary power.

---

## End Note

[1] Swaab, D.F., Garcia-Falgueras, A. (2009), "Sexual differentiation of the human brain in relation to gender identity and sexual orientation," *Functional Neurology* 24 (1), pp.17-28.

---

## Reference

Nicolosi, J. (1991, 2020) *Reparative Therapy of Male Homosexuality.* Tarzana, CA: Liberal Mind Publishers.

## Chapter Twenty-Five

# The Double-Loop Experience

The central healing process of Reparative Therapy® is what we call the "Double Loop Experience." In this process, an accurately attuned, empathic therapist helps the client re-experience the feelings that have split apart his psyche, so that he can reconnect with those renounced parts of himself. The split-off parts of the self have, we find, often been renounced because of conscious and unconscious feelings of shame.

### Intimacy, not Eroticism

A particular benefit of the Double Loop experience for many men is that it assures them that an emotional connection with another man need not be "gay," and that feelings of tenderness and vulnerability that come up through this connection with another man are healing, affirmative and non-erotic.

The most powerful transformative moment is when the client re-experiences an early trauma, while emotionally present in the inter-subjective moment of the Double Loop. It is through this connectedness with the therapist that the client is able to feel the bodily sensations that are associated with his painful early experiences. The greatest healing moments occur when the client can feel what seems to be unbearable feeling, while at the same moment, experiencing the care, encouragement, and understanding of the therapist.

The client's communication—the "putting into words" of his feelings—is not just a cognitive act, but an act of trust that such a thing is possible, and that it can be experienced without psychic disintegration. It is this *trust* that enables unification between the client's left and right brain hemispheres; between cognitive and affective; and between conscious and unconscious—all through the medium of the body, while in contact with the therapist.

In the Double Loop Experience, the client receives the therapist's expression of respect and esteem on a *feeling* level, not just a *thinking* level, which results in his experience of feeling deeply known and understood. At its best, this moment is reminiscent of the earliest attunement that was felt between mother and infant child.

## Dissipation of Shame through Exposure

Shame is what blocks the homosexually oriented man from living in the Assertive Stance. The Double Loop experience is the most powerful tool available for disempowering the inhibitory effect of shame. Shame dissipates best through exposure, which is the process for which the Double Loop is ideally suited.

Internally, shame is an inhibitor of emotional expression, a "shut-down" state. Most shame moments center around experiences of a deep feeling of gender inferiority. The therapeutic goal is for the client to sit in the shame—including the feelings that surround and underlie it—while he experiences contact with the understanding and accepting therapist.

The Double Loop experience of psychotherapy is a uniquely human event between two people in time, and contains a sort of mystical or transpersonal quality with a surreal edge to it. When the client drops his usual defenses, the Double Loop offers a transformative depth of emotional exchange.

As the True Self gradually begins to emerge, no longer constricted by illusions and distortions, and no longer bound in the straitjacket of the False Self, we see a markedly greater outflow of energy in relating to others, and far less protective self-preoccupation.

## Chapter Twenty-Six

# What If I Don't Change?

Over the years, many men have come to my office for help; homosexuality doesn't work in their lives. It just never feels right or true. To these men, it is clear that gay relationships don't reflect who they are as gendered beings, and they believe that they have been designed—physically and emotionally—for opposite-sex coupling.

But Reparative Therapy is a long and difficult process, with no guarantee of success. What if the man doesn't change? Will he have gained anything of value?

People are often surprised to hear that in Reparative Therapy, typically there is very little discussion about sex. In fact, it is a mistake for any psychotherapy to focus exclusively on one particular symptom. Clients come in with a difficulty that they want removed from their life—an eating disorder, gambling obsession, or unwanted same-sex attraction—but good therapy addresses the whole person.

I typically tell my clients in the very first session, "Rule Number One is, never accept anything I say unless it resonates as true for you." The experience of the client, whatever that may be, must always trump any preconceived theory.

Reparative theory holds that the origin of SSA is in unmet emotional and identification needs with the same sex, and the client is free to accept or reject that premise. If that doesn't feel true to him, he will usually decide to leave therapy after one or two sessions.

Through a relationship with an attuned therapist, the client discovers how it feels to emotionally disclose to another man—revealing those long-buried, shame-evoking feelings. He experiences from him a deep acceptance of wherever he is in his life, at that point in time, whether he changes or not. Such an experience is always deeply therapeutic.

Besides an enhanced ability to develop genuine male friendships, the client will discover healthier relationships with females—where he learns to prohibit the boundary violations with women that have caused him to surrender his separate, masculine selfhood.

But what about the client who fails to change; will he be left in a sort of "intimacy limbo"—not heterosexual, yet unable to be intimate with men? The truth is, our client was never *intimate* with men. That is why he came to therapy. He also came to us because he believes that true sexual intimacy with a person of the same gender is, in fact, not possible: same-sex eroticism simply fails to match his biological and emotional design, and does not reflect who he is on the deepest level.

Other men enter Reparative Therapy as gay-identified from the start. With those clients, we agree on a precondition to our working together—that is, we will not address the issue of sexual-identity change, but we will work on all of their other problems in living. And so we work on issues like capacity for intimacy, problems with self-esteem, internalized shame, childhood trauma, and the search for identity.

Some of our clients decide to change course and embrace homosexuality as "who they are." Others never lose their conviction that they were designed to be heterosexual, and they persist toward that goal. Still others remain ambivalent about change, while going in and out of gay life over a period of months or years. We accept their choices even if we don't agree with them, because we accept the person.

## Chapter Twenty-Seven

# Why I Am Not a Neutral Therapist

> *"How could I have been designed by my creator for homosexuality?" the client asked.*

A client once told me about his experience with another psychologist. This psychologist told him that he, the client, was born gay, and said that his unwanted attractions (whether he liked it or not) revealed "who he really was."

The client asked if he could be referred to a different therapist who would help him explore the possibility of change. The psychologist (who, it turned out, was gay) said, "No. I won't participate in something unethical. This denial of your homosexuality is a reflection of your self-hatred. *There is no other valid position on this issue*!"

In these politically correct times, where diversity of thought is so restricted, psychologists who see heterosexuality as the norm are extremely reticent to speak up.

On another occasion, a Christian psychologist contacted me to discuss reorientation therapy for SSA men. Hoping to find a politically "safe" compromise with the American Psychological Association, he was anxious to avoid value judgments and to remain noncommittal about the validity of homosexuality. The solution, he thought, would be a simple behavior modification program.

Speaking from my 25 years of experience in this field, I told him I found his approach naive and ultimately unworkable. Our men do not come to us just to change their unwanted behavior. They come to us to change their sense of self—to *be* more heterosexual, not just to "act" heterosexually; to feel comfortable in relationships with straight men, to learn to hold onto their masculine autonomy with women—in short, to fulfill their latent heterosexual potential. A barebones behavior-modification program might be politically safe, but because of its shallowness, it would inevitably fail.

The developmental model we suggest must deeply resonate with the men we work with, or they will (rightfully) leave our office and pursue a different therapeutic approach. We explain that our position differs from the American Psychological Association, which sees homosexuality and heterosexuality as equivalent, and along the way, we encourage them to clarify and reclarify the direction of their identity commitment. The alternative, now mainstream approach—gay-affirmative therapy—should, of course, be available as an alternative for any such client.

Philosophically, I am an essentialist—not a social constructionist: I believe that gender identity and sexual orientation are grounded in biological reality. The body tells us who we are, and we cannot "construct"—assemble or disassemble—a different reality in which gender and sexual identity are out of synchrony with biology.

The belief that humanity is designed for heterosexuality has been shaped by age-old religious and cultural forces, which must be respected as a welcome aspect of intellectual diversity. Our belief is not a "phobia" or pathological fear.

Natural-law philosophy says this view derives from mankind's *collective, intuitive knowledge*; a sort of natural, instinctive conscience. This would explain why so many people—even the nonreligious—sense that a gay identity is a false construct.

In fact, the very man who was instrumental in getting homosexuality removed from the list of mental disorders, psychiatrist Robert Spitzer, told us in an interview (published several years ago by NARTH at www.narth.com), that in homosexuality, "something's not working." This is a thought-provoking admission from the man whose life's work in the psychiatric profession resulted in the normalization of homosexuality.

Again, in an interview with the German Institute for Youth and Society, Spitzer said, when asked about the normality of homosexuality, "*. . . intuitively, I think that 'something is not working.'*"

Many years later, as society increasingly welcomed homosexuality, Spitzer, under growing pressure from gay activists, backtracked on some of the conclusions of his study of change.

In spite of Spitzer's ambivalence about change, the vast majority of clients who come to us are convinced that SSA has been maladaptive in their lives. Their impetus for change comes from their deep conviction that, underneath it all, they really are heterosexual men, and they seek a therapist who sees their inner potential and will help them activate it.

## Chapter Twenty-Eight

# A Shared Delight

In my search for the particular quality of father-son bonding that is fundamental to the development of the boy's masculine identity, I have been led to a phenomenon that I call "a shared delight."

I am convinced that the healthy development of masculine identification depends on this phenomenon. This special emotional exchange should be between the boy and his father, although a father figure or grandfather may serve the purpose where no father is available. It is not a single event or one-time occurrence, but should characterize the relationship.

This particular style of emotional attunement is especially important during the critical developmental gender-identity period.

Homosexual men have great difficulty recalling childhood father-son activities that were exciting and enjoyable and included success and achievement—a shared delight. They typically do not have many positive memories of their fathers coaching them to gain a new skill that involves bodily activity or strength. Indeed, many lament this deprivation.

An example of "a shared delight" is found in writer and social commentator Malcolm Muggeridge's autobiography. Malcolm's father was his hero; and as a teenager, Malcolm would travel to his father's office in London. When he arrived, he noticed an embodied shift in his father:

> *When he saw me, his face always lit up, as it had a way of doing, quite suddenly, thereby completely altering his appearance; transforming him from a rather cavernous, shrunken man into someone boyish and ardent. He would leap agilely off his stool, wave gaily to his colleague—and we would make off together.*
>
> *There was always about these excursions an element of being on an illicit spree, which greatly added to their pleasure. They were the most enjoyable episodes in all my childhood.*

As we work with men who experience same-sex attractions, we hear that repeated theme—their inability to recall "a shared delight."

Physical interaction between father and son is essential in making the father feel familiar, non-mysterious, and completely approachable in the boy's eyes. So much of what lies behind adult same-sex attraction is that deep, lingering, unsatisfied desire for physical closeness with a man. With internalization of the father's masculinity, there will be no need for the client to sexualize another man.

## Chapter Twenty-Nine

# Some Thoughts on the Boy Scouts

*The problem is not about admitting homosexual boys; it's about the transmission of an ideology.*

Homosexually oriented boys are now admitted into the Boy Scouts. Is this a wise policy for youth groups? "Yes," I've often said, "because boys with same-sex attractions can benefit greatly from male bonding experiences."

Then what is the source of the conflict?

Youth groups provide an important rite of passage for boys growing into manhood. In fact, the Boy Scouts of America (BSA) never did exclude same-sex attracted members—their policy was "don't ask, don't tell," like the policy once held by the military.

That worked well until gay activists insisted that boys should enter the Scouts with a "*gay is who I am*" mentality.

When this issue was being debated, gay activists successfully played it to the press that the BSA was discriminating against homosexual boys—that they didn't want them.

But the BSA should have fought for what they really stood for: that all boys are welcome, but that the Scouts would continue to promote the Judeo-Christian understanding of human identity and biological design.

People with this Judeo-Christian worldview see a gay identity as a superficial layer of someone's personal identity. They see homosexuality as evidence of trauma . . . as a problematic attraction . . . as a chosen identity that is disconnected from biological reality. The same is true of transgendered boys. A person's truest and deepest identity must be grounded in his biological sex, which then puts him in harmony with his design. This is the worldview shared by traditional Christians, traditional Jews, Muslims, and Baha'i, among other faiths. Their worldview cannot simply be discounted as "prejudice" rooted in "animosity." People of traditional faith are confident that on a deeper, truer level, these boys were created to live out their biological design.

Gay activists however, believe that a gay identity *must* be accepted by everyone *as representing that particular person's inborn nature.*

The traditional view is not an easy concept to argue, in an age where every individual is said to be free to "choose" his own identity— male, female, non-binary gender, "questioning," bisexual, gay or straight. In today's world, it seems like a slap in the face to tell someone, "This *can't* be who you really are."

## The Problem of Gay Scout Leaders

What's going to happen with the Scout policy of accepting gay-identified Scout leaders? What will you say when you see a gay leader encouraging the boys to "discover who they are" with the idea that they, too, may be gay? Because this will inevitably happen.

One could argue that the BSA is asexual. They don't talk about sex. They're not allowed to.

*But this issue is not about sex—it's about the transmission of an ideology.* When gay activists get into positions of Scout leadership, they will, naturally, want to serve as role models. They will be on a mission to insist that homosexuality is the same as heterosexuality. They'll talk about their belief that children don't need two married biological parents. They'll introduce the boys to their partner or "husband." They will present their lives as examples, and themselves as role models.

That approach will teach *not* just that this particular, individual Scout leader has qualities to emulate (which no doubt is true; the gay Scout leader may have many good character qualities), but it mixes up the example of his personal character with his homosexuality, and sends the message that *homosexuality itself* is good.

Our culture has caved in on this issue; our schools, our youth organizations, the media, movies, government—the psychological and medical professions—everywhere; the new accepted view is that the traditional understanding of human identity can only be "hatred." Almost no one is left to speak the truth about human design and purpose.

For people of traditional faith, new Scouting alternatives have been created. One good alternative to investigate is Trail Life USA.

## Chapter Thirty

# The Bob Spitzer I Knew

*by Linda Ames Nicolosi*

*The man may be a hero to the gay community, yet he retained an intuitive sense that something is missing in homosexuality.*

When I opened the newspaper a couple of days after Christmas in 2015, I was surprised to see a familiar face in the obituaries section: psychiatrist Robert Spitzer. The name brought back a flood of personal memories. I had learned something about human nature from Bob Spitzer, and also about politics as they play out behind the scenes in the mental-health establishment.

About 15 years before, Spitzer had asked me to help him with a new research project he was working on—a study of people who had come out of a gay lifestyle. He needed help on his wording and the expression of concepts, and I was, at the time, Publications Director for NARTH (National Association for Research and Therapy of Homosexuality).

I was flattered to be trusted with the job. Dr. Spitzer was one of the most celebrated psychiatrists of recent memory. This celebrity was not because of his reputation as a clinician; it was because he had been instrumental in the pivotal 1973 decision to remove homosexuality from the *Diagnostic and Statistical Manual*, a change which elites in our culture had been clamoring for.

And so began an almost daily email correspondence with Spitzer that lasted for several months. As the cultural hero who had supposedly "normalized" homosexuality, he would be, I thought, one of the foremost experts on the subject.

But I was in for a surprise. Not only did Spitzer know very little about homosexuality and the actual work of a clinician (a subject which he seemed to have little interest in studying) but he had also minimal knowledge of, or—apparently—interest in, psycho-dynamic psychology. That shouldn't have been a shock: his specialty at Columbia University was biometrics, and his work on the psychiatric manual was to master the tricky job of defining and categorizing hundreds of disorders and pseudo-disorders—an ever-changing jigsaw puzzle of semantics.

But Spitzer was, no doubt, a truly compassionate man, and he was proud that through the 1973 decision, he had helped free LGB people from cultural oppression. But when he called me in 2001 (he was then in the fading years of his career), I sensed that a feeling of guilt was nagging at him. For one thing, he did not like the pressure within the psychiatric establishment to stop clinicians from helping patients who were unhappy with their same-sex attractions. ("Patients should have the right," he told me in an interview, "to explore their heterosexual potential.")

And, like most psychiatrists, as Spitzer explained in an interview published in the NARTH Bulletin in 2001, "I thought that homosexual behavior could not be resisted . . . that no one could really change their orientation. I now believe that's untrue—some people can and do change."

Spitzer's history made him a highly improbable figure as the champion of ex-gays. In fact, some of the older psychoanalysts who had treated patients for homosexuality warned NARTH not to cooperate with him; Dr. Charles Socarides, in particular, harbored a deep resentment toward Spitzer and insisted that he could not be trusted to interview any NARTH clinician's former patients—he called his old rival a "snake in the grass."

Nonetheless, Spitzer's study found 200 subjects, and went forward. Change was found not to be complete and absolute; a person didn't simply "switch orientations"; their success was best described as "a reduction in homosexual attractions and an increase in heterosexual attractions." But "good heterosexual functioning" was reportedly achieved in 67% of the men who had rarely or never felt any heterosexual attraction. Nearly all the subjects said they now felt more comfortable with their biologically appropriate gender.

Spitzer's conclusion was, wisely, a cautious and qualified one, because change (as with alcoholism, obesity, and drug problems) is notoriously hard. All he said was this: "Contrary to conventional wisdom, some highly motivated individuals, using a variety of change efforts, can make substantial change in multiple indicators of sexual orientation, and achieve good heterosexual functioning."

But even that qualified conclusion was too much for the LGB establishment. Fresh from recent cultural victories, this was a shocking betrayal; coming from a onetime ally, it had to be punished.

Spitzer was clearly taken aback by the ugliness of the pre-publication reaction. His social group, as he explained, was not the evangelical Christians who were most often the subjects in his study, but a different demographic, as he explained to me: the "readers of the *New York Times*."

Still, he seemed unable to comprehend that he could be an enemy of anyone for discovering this neglected population of ex-gays. I think he believed that support for any community that was culturally marginalized would be—as it once had been—a popular move, even among New York's cultural elite. This time, however, he had misjudged the temper of the times; he had failed to recognize the "new orthodoxy" and its changing concept of victimology.

Just before the study was due to be published, I received this S.O.S. call from him, after he was barraged with vitriol from gay activists: "I have been reviewing the emails that I have received, and I must admit I had the fantasy of giving up this whole thing . . . !"

## Politics and Science as Bedfellows

This turn of events was alarming. I considered his new study to be a needed corrective in the scientific literature, and I didn't want him to back out. I told him so. But he was worried about what his colleagues would think. They were warning him about what the study might do (a study which had nothing to do with people who were happily gay!) to hurt the forward march of gay activism.

He wrote back, "Sorry to frighten you. My main concern—other than what this whole thing does to my reputation in the scientific community—is that the effect of this study is to help 5,000 ex-gays or potential ex-gays . . . [while] I have seriously hurt five million gays."

But if the study told the truth, why should Spitzer think about "who would be hurt"? Was consideration of "who would be hurt" (or in this case, "who would dislike the results") something that had propelled him to de-list homosexuality as a disorder in the first place? He was a scientist. Shouldn't he be ashamed of himself, to be worrying about who wouldn't like the results?

Those years were the beginning of a long, punishing barrage of attacks on Spitzer from the gay community. Further, there began a new embrace of Spitzer by evangelicals—who, of course, are not the sort of folks thought very attractive by the readers of the *New York Times*. It was an embrace which he found embarrassing. He made a number of attempts to publicly distance himself from the evangelical community.

Now that the study was over and had attracted so much vitriol, the evangelicals (and I myself) no longer had his ear. Instead, Spitzer was now having monthly lunches in New York with Jack Drescher, a gay-activist psychiatrist and a bitter opponent of sexual-orientation change efforts. Although Spitzer had once said, "I miss our daily email exchanges," now that the heat was really on for him, I did not hear from him much anymore. Was Jack Drescher now the man who had the power to influence his beliefs?

Seems likely. "The fact that gay marriage is allowed today is in part owed to Bob Spitzer," Drescher later told BBC News in a warm tribute in Spitzer's obituary.

Those years after Spitzer's study was published must have been difficult ones. Eventually, Spitzer would no longer answer any email from me. He now wanted the editor of the journal to retract his study, but no such request was granted.

After all, in the years subsequent to the study, he had uncovered no new data; he had simply come to fear that many of his original subjects might have either been lying or self-deluded.

The public collapse (and theological reversal) of the leadership of Exodus Ministries surely had added to Spitzer's embarrassment. And, there was the growing cultural and religious shift toward a full and enthusiastic embrace of homosexuality. Spitzer's study had marked the man as no longer *avant garde*, but in fact behind-the-times. He seemed mortified, later describing that study as "the one thing" he regretted in his long career.

Indeed, Spitzer had an ideological "center" that was hard to put a finger on. He was a self-described "atheist and evolutionist," telling me in one of our email debates, "The concept of sin or divine purpose means nothing to me. However, the concept of design in evolution means a lot." If his son were homosexual, he said, he would hope he would seek therapy for it, and "I would hope that his motivation for change would be an intuitive sense that his life would be better and more fulfilling if he fully utilized his heterosexual potential."

He added, "Heterosexuality is—generally—a more satisfying condition than homosexuality." Furthermore, when I described him in an article as "the man who had normalized homosexuality," he insisted on a correction. "I never 'normalized' homosexuality," he said, adding, rather obtusely, "I merely de-listed it as a disorder."

In a letter written to an ex-lesbian, Spitzer had expressed an almost wistful respect for her Christian faith. He said, "What has been wonderful to me about participating in this study is understanding, in a way that I never did before this study, how deeply religious people . . . experience the world and their life. I suppose I would be happier if I could have that perspective, particularly now that I have a potentially disabling brain disorder." (Spitzer had just been diagnosed with Parkinson's.) "But to me, religion and the notion of an afterlife and divine intervention or guidance is just . . . wishful thinking to avoid the true state of affairs. There is no divine guidance or afterlife. I don't need Scripture to know that certain behavior is harmful to self or others."

So, back in 1973, did Spitzer "discover" through study of the clinical data—as the public believed at the time that he had done, and still incorrectly believes—that homosexuality had been found to be normal? Not only did he specifically deny normalizing the condition, but

I still have his words which suggest a dim awareness of "the law that is written on the heart"—of those things that one "can't not know" unless that awareness has been somehow erased. "In homosexuality," he had said, "something's not working."

Strange words from a hero to the gay world.

## Chapter Thirty-One

# "Homosexuality Is Against Art"

*by Linda Ames Nicolosi*

Eli Siegel's "Aesthetic Realism" is a philosophy that offers a window into the nature of homosexuality from an artistic perspective. Siegel was an award-winning poet as well as a philosopher with a small but devoted band of followers. He died in 1978. His work drew a clear connection between homosexuality and narcissism.

"Being homosexual is not your problem," Siegel tells his students. "The way you see the world is inaccurate. As that changes, the homosexual situation will change . . . . Sameness and difference is what homosexuality doesn't sufficiently honor."

In the family structure which is most common among gay men, mother and son form a bond of specialness, Siegel notes, which constricts the boy's true nature and excludes the father. Such a relationship produces, in the son, both anger and love toward the mother.

This, Siegel notes, results in the boy's feeling of "adoring contempt"; forever after, women are experienced as "boring," "uninteresting pushovers," and "easy conquests."

As one student of Aesthetic Realism explained, the homosexual man "robs a woman of dimension . . . [H]e gushes over her, while he contemptuously dismisses her."

The distorted mother-son relationship affects all the boy's future relationships and eventually forms him as a homosexual. The conquest of his mother was too easy, Siegel says; in adulthood, he then desires to repeat that victory with someone whom he sees as stronger—a man. This way, "he can have the triumph of seeing that strong person melt."

Aesthetic Realism draws its principles from the worlds of ethics and art. It calls homosexuality "ugly" and "against art" because it fails to make one out of opposites. Owing to the fact that homosexuality "fosters contempt," it is unethical, Siegel charges, and therefore "unjust" to the world.

Aesthetic Realism in some ways parallels the Judeo-Christian understanding of homosexuality. Both Jewish and Christian traditions stress the beauty, necessity and naturalness of gender complementarity. Both stress that the purpose of life is self-giving—"loving the world" as Siegel terms it—or, in a psychoanalytic sense, growing out of one's childhood narcissism. Joseph Nicolosi's own original article on Aesthetic Realism has been lost, but most of that earlier article's observations are recaptured here. The family structure that his Reparative Therapy identified as the "Triadic Narcissistic Relationship" is vividly portrayed in Siegel's students' testimonies.

The following are statements by Eli Siegel on homosexuality:

[Siegel to a student:] "Being homosexual is not your problem. The way you see the world is inaccurate. As that changes, the homosexual situation will change. You made some bad philosophical and ethical choices at an early age which have to be revoked . . . you've had this superstructure so long, you think it is 'you.' I don't think it is."

"As one learns from Aesthetic Realism to see the world justly . . . homosexuality simply, logically and deeply changes."

"When the homosexual love that is sought for is understood—when its motive is understood—that love has no longer the charm that it seemed to have."

"Mothers [of homosexuals] tend to foster a feeling of glory in their male child. A good way for a mother to increase her own glory, is to make her son as important as he can be. The desire for superiority is the other side of the desire to have as much contempt for other people as possible."

"Homosexuality has a preponderant tendency to love of oneself and making the outside world a minor matter."

"The feeling of romance fades more quickly in homosexual love than elsewhere; and the feeling about another's body . . . also fades quickly."

In a dialogue with a student, Siegel told him that he had his "greatest love affair very early" with his mother, who lived for him; and he—the son—was "the one mooring point in her life; otherwise her vessel was lost." It gave him "a terrific feeling of importance."

Yet, Siegel notes this irony: the child is unfree in the relationship because of its narcissistic entanglement; he "finds early that the good mood of his mother depends on the contributions to her happiness he chooses to make."

He observes that sex in a gay relationship often results in "a dim, annoying vacuity," because it does not allow for true emotional connection. He says the self is a "to-be-known" reality, and without it, depression sets in, which is "a dull, basic tragedy."

Siegel was blunt in confronting his students. He challenged one man as follows:

[Siegel:] "Do you think there can still be love between your mother and father?"

[Student:] "My father is not capable of showing emotions."

[Siegel:] "He got married and welcomed the outside world as different, which is something *you've* not been able to do."

One of his students reported: "As I changed from homosexuality, I felt this loneliness—which I had taken for granted as part of human nature—lift from me like a thick blanket . . . . Mr. Siegel has enabled something inside me—dim, stagnant and buried away—to come alive."

And so we are reminded that homosexuality is not just the realm of the psychotherapist and the minister, but also, of the philosopher and the artist. They, too, see the wisdom and beauty in the unity of opposites.

---

## Reference

Reiss, Ellen, ed. (1986) *The Aesthetic Realism of Eli Siegel and the Change from Homosexuality.* N.Y.: 1986, Definition Press.)

## Chapter Thirty-Two

# In Conclusion

*—by Linda A. Nicolosi*

Throughout this book, we have seen what male homosexuality is: an interruption of the identification and attachment process.

This breach leaves the boy with an unresolved need for male attention, affection and approval that becomes eroticized.

The man who develops homosexually is seeking a way to get close to other men, to merge with them, to "feel" with them, and to break down the emotional barriers of isolation, shame and masculine disempowerment.

But the man who *sees the truth about homosexuality*, and is motivated to live authentically, can learn to meet his longings for same-sex love in brotherly and non-erotic ways. He sees that:

— Homosexuality undermines the camaraderie of a group of men who work together toward a common goal; on the battlefield, at work, or any place where there is a shared effort. Masculine teamwork is beautiful in its frankness, directness, and trust. Truly, "iron sharpens iron," strengthening each man through the male bond; but this intimacy is contaminated when there is an undercurrent of homoeroticism. Homosexuality means all the man's peers become potential sex partners.

— Homosexuality is inherently narcissistic. Two men are erotically drawn to someone like themselves because of a deficit. They were made for the love of differentness, but they cannot love difference because they have experienced defensive detachment against the internalization of the maleness that should have been theirs.

— Each man, in loving the other man, is trying to love himself as he should have been loved during a critical development period. When two men come together in a gay partnership, neither their bodies nor their psyches "fit." They are forced to negotiate a sexual contact that involves a "my-turn-your-turn" distortion represented by anal sex and oral sex. Anal sex, in particular, is degrading, unclean,and physically damaging. Heterosexuality, in contrast, is not a narcissistic turning-inward, but an expansive outward-seeking toward the other person and toward new life.

— Sex that involves the organ of defecation *defeats* the greatest wonder in human existence—a man and a woman's participation in creation. Sodomy is a barren and meaningless act, separating a man from his biological lineage. If he wants children, he must hire an outsider to carry his child, which in turn, cuts off that mother from her own biological offspring.

— Two males will always be rivals. We see a reflection of this aspect of nature in the animal world; male wolves in a pack will never be at peace with one another, but will test each other for dominance. Yet a female wolf will live with a male in relative peace, because she does not belong to the same dominance hierarchy; she and the male are not made by nature to be rivals. And so it is not surprising that gay male relationships are plagued by rivalry, instability, and, not infrequently, physical violence.

— The bringing together of two men results in a relationship that is almost always unfaithful. While the partners may negotiate an agreement to live together as mutual friends, studies show that the agreement to have outside affairs is typical. Gay researchers have even found that if this agreement to have outside sexual escapades is ***not*** made, the relationship will not endure. To justify their infidelity, gay apologists redefine "fidelity" to mean just "emotional faithfulness" rather than sexual faithfulness, thus splitting off the man's emotions from his body. There is an effort now by gay activists in the American Psychological Association to "de-stigmatize" promiscuity, especially gay promiscuity, and to try to force society to grant it cultural legitimacy.

— Gay male life is inherently unmoored and undisciplined. Gay men tend to see erotic energy everywhere; it runs like an electric current throughout their daily lives. There is an adolescent obsession with sex and other men's sex organs. Without the natural grounding effect of a woman in a relationship, this immaturity is not surprising.

— Growing up unanchored in his own body, the gay man inevitably sees gender in a distorted way. He seeks validation of his distorted vision by pushing society into celebrating his distortion. Thus, he will fight for the normalizing of transgenderism as well as homosexuality. He understands very well what it feels like to be unanchored in one's natural gender and so he will push for society's rejection of natural, traditional, complementary sex roles. Thus he seeks to justify his distortion, which gnaws at him on some deep level as not true and not authentic.

— Gender distortion pulls civilization into an anything-goes pansexualism, instead of reinforcing the boundaries that are necessary to civilizational order. Philosopher/historians Will and Ariel Durant observe that sex is a "river of fire that must be banked and cooled by a hundred restraints." To restrain this river of fire, natural marriage between a man and a woman has been civilization's bulwark. When one civilizational boundary falls, we see a blurring of the other essential separations between adult and child, mentor and mentee, even a shattering of the dividing line between sacred and profane.

— The gay man's relationships with women are as distorted as his relationships with men. He often has a female "best friend," typically a narcissistic woman who enjoys the flattering attention of a "neutered" man who will help her in the kitchen and listen to her complaints about her husband. She doesn't know that in using the man this way, she disrespects his masculine dignity. And while the man enjoys this flattering intimacy as a woman's best friend, which hearkens back to the feeling of specialness he had with his mother, he secretly harbors contempt for her and resents her emasculating power. In his distorted way of thinking, women are all too familiar, while men are exciting, unfathomable and exotic.

— Gay men carry a deep grievance against straight men, having felt excluded by their fathers and their male peers. We often see them allying themselves with feminist political causes; in this way, they can "get back at" powerful men in the same manner that they allied themselves with their mothers against their fathers. "Macho" and narcissistic men are especially disliked. There is a motivation to "out" other men as secretly gay and "just like me." In their sexual lives, many gay men seek to reenact (and thus, somehow "master") these long-felt feelings of powerlessness and rage in acts of S&M and sexual bondage. A surprising number seek the perverse thrill of being shamed by being discovered in acts of public sex.

## This is Not a "Scientific" Disagreement

How is it that homosexuality is seen so differently by different people? The difference cannot be settled by science, because, ultimately, the dispute is not scientific, but ideological. Therefore, it will be seen through the lens of one's life philosophy. How a person resolves the dispute will depend on which lens he views it through.

Secular-progressives believe humanity evolved from purposeless processes and that we have no fixed "human nature." They see man as naturally good, and as free to reinvent himself.

Traditionalists believe the opposite—creation is good, yet we are also inherently flawed. We were designed for a purpose by a creator, and we have a fixed human nature with which we must live in harmony in order to find true peace. According to that view, homosexuality is inevitably unnatural.

So what is the answer to the question of homosexuality? When one sees that homosexuality is not chosen, but also that it is not good for the individual or society, tolerance is the best compromise—to *tolerate* but not to *affirm,* knowing that it is a condition that arises from deep, genuine and understandable inner longings.

Yet at the same time, we also hold to the conviction that growth into fullest manhood is never beyond any man's reach.

## Addendum I:

# Two Case Stories

*By David Pickup, M.A., LMFT*

*Clinician David Pickup worked as a trainee under Dr. Joseph Nicolosi before starting his own practice in Texas. Here, he offers two client stories which use many of Dr. Nicolosi's theoretical concepts and techniques. The names have been changed.*

## CASE STORY NO. 1: THERAPY WITH A TEENAGER

Sixteen-year-old Stan walked into my office one day with his father. He and his family were from Mississippi, with a long history of football champions in the family. Stan, who had inherited the family talent for sports, was expected to be the best champion of them all.

Stan's father, Chuck, had made the therapy appointment only a few days before, after the boy had told his parents he was sure he was gay. His father was clearly panicked; homosexuality was the very thing he had always tried to prevent during Stan's entire upbringing.

But as a therapist, my first concern with a minor is whether he really wants to be in therapy, instead of being forced into it by his parents. So I asked Stan if he really wanted to be there, and I wanted to know what he believed in terms of gender and sexuality. This distressed boy looked at me through anxious eyes saying he wasn't sure, and he didn't know what to do. The heartbreak coming from this kid was palpable.

I looked straight at him and told him that he didn't have to be here, and that real therapy is not about forcing anything on anyone. I told him I wasn't about to judge him, and that if he felt he might be gay, then he had every right to decide that matter for himself. It was up to him to decide if he believed that this condition was innate, or if underlying issues were causing his attractions.

For what was probably the first time in his life, Stan's anxiety began to settle down because another man who might play a significant role in his life, was telling him he wouldn't condemn him.

I then asked Stan if he would tell me about his feelings and how long he had been dealing with sexuality issues. He told me he had felt low self-esteem since grade school, and then described what had happened between him and his parents, and in his peer relationships. And finally, he told me about his sexual attractions for other guys. It all began to tumble out.

This boy had been terrified, closed off emotionally, and had been putting on a false "good-little-boy" face since he was five. He was very talented at sports, but nothing, it seems, was ever good enough for his father. His dad, Chuck, would brook no nonsense if Stan made even simple errors in practice or games. If Stan looked discouraged, he would rip him apart with shame to ensure he would be successful the next time. This tactic was designed to push him into always being at the top of his game—always ensuring his manhood, always preventing any homosexual leanings.

Of course, one way to mishandle a fundamental issue with one's child is to react in a dramatic way—in anger, while angrily laying out consequences.

Over the years at home, the shaming would continue with a constant barrage of emotional traps that involved putting Stan in double-binds, in which he couldn't win or get approval, whether or not he accepted Dad's upbraiding. If the boy did not accept the discipline, he was shamed for his rebellion. If he did (outwardly) accept the discipline, he would then shut down emotionally inside.

## A Father-Son Mismatch

Some boys are tough enough to endure Stan's father's approach. This teenager, however, like so many of our same-sex attracted clients, was emotionally sensitive. There was a father-son temperamental mismatch that had disrupted the male identification process. As a result of this hurt, Stan rejected his normal and healthy need for male love, which meant he would later seek to find that love and understanding from another man, instead of internalizing it within himself through the normal identification process.

Dr. Joseph Nicolosi and some other clinicians have described this unconscious developmental process as "defensive detachment." In other words, the child decides, unconsciously, "You, my dad, have hurt me, so I reject you and the masculinity you represent."

In later sessions, more and more information came out about how impossible the father-son relationship had been for at least the last ten years. I also learned that Chuck's emotional reaction was so explosive upon Stan's revelation of his sexuality, that Chuck tackled his son to the floor and told him he couldn't possibly be gay. The boy was so terrified that he bolted out of the house down a country road and into the night without his shoes, running far away from home.

More stories were revealed to me about how at various times, Dad would insist that Stan hug him while Stan talked about his impermissible feelings—feelings of the sort that could result in a beating. That put the boy in a double bind. His dad's behavior was so abusive that it required me to contact Child Protective Services. The man would constantly, albeit unconsciously, put Stan in shame-based disciplinary situations "for his own good," while wanting Stan to be affectionate at the same time. Can you imagine demanding emotional and physical affection while putting your son in a vice-like grip of shame in order to make him a manly football player?

After years of this treatment, Stan began to engage in physically cutting himself in an unconscious attempt to express his anguish and self-hatred.

The key to helping Stan resume his growth into manhood was for me, and hopefully, other men in his life, to offer unconditional love without judgment, without putting him into traps from which there was no escape; to listen to him, no matter what his feelings were—even feelings about other boys, about Dad, about Mother, about his sexuality . . . anything he needed to talk about. It was this kind of authentic relationship that he received in therapy—evidently, for the first time in his life—that allowed Stan to speak from his core emotions. This authentic connection between Stan and myself then led then to the gradual freeing of his own authentic self.

Stan began to talk openly of how it felt to be attracted to other guys, who were mostly his age, that he could get approval from, and also experience the male affection for which he ached.

Over time, Stan also discovered a chronic sense of inferiority inside of himself underneath all his homosexual feelings. This is a key to understanding homosexual feelings—he had to feel inferior about himself in order to feel erotically attracted to another boy. This profound revelation, which came through his own awareness, sent him into a healing state of deep grief. Such a healing is what happens to us all, whatever our issues, when we go through a healthy grieving process.... *We see the rise of the authentic and mature self.* This process is restorative for all human beings when it leads to self-compassion and to discovery of the truth about our lives' most formative experiences.

## Finding His Masculine Wholeness

Slowly, Stan began to feel a release from his internal double binds. Dad was taught, in therapy, how to relate much better to his son. Stan began to feel the wonderful experience of his own masculine wholeness in his own body as he learned how to stand up for himself. He learned the power of authenticity and self-confidence, not just in his thoughts, but in that deep place that other men who have had less traumatic life experiences are apt to take for granted. It is an assertion felt in their own bodies, right near the center of their chests where their hearts live. He liked how this felt, and he smiled after these revelations. Stan also learned about setting healthy boundaries with both his parents, and he saw that relationships could be better and more connected when boundaries were in place.

Gradually, the more Stan resolved his shame-based ideas of himself, the more he moved into authenticity and confidence, the more he simply let himself feel his feelings—yes, even the homosexual ones when they arose, without shaming himself. This allowed his homoerotic impulses to naturally lessen.

After a couple of years of intense therapy, Stan rarely has homosexual feelings any more, and he's becoming interested in relationships with girls. But coming out of homosexuality is, as all ex-gay men know, a lifetime process, requiring the ongoing fulfillment of normal, male affectional needs without eroticism.

## Change Cannot Be Forced

Stan may continue to feel some degree of homosexual feelings, or he may not. But in terms of merely feeling his feelings, who cares? "Who we are" in the deepest sense is much more than our passing erotic responses. Stan has now exclaimed how good it feels to be a man, and his depression and anxiety have greatly lessened.

For years, Stan had experienced so many undeserved traumas. And yet, heroically, he kept going through it all. I had to ensure he had every opportunity to heal and change in the relationship with his own father if at all possible, because if I, as his mentor and therapist, had tried to continue to be a "father" to him myself, this would potentially be harmful. I had to release him from our time in therapy for his greater good. And that is both difficult and loving at the same time.

Here's the news most of the world does not understand: When a man feels good about his own manhood at his deep core of identity, it's almost impossible to eroticize the male body. It's the difference between objectifying maleness, and feeling maleness as a *subjectively fulfilling experience* which one does not need to seek outside oneself.

Good therapy for unwanted homosexuality is founded on the belief that homosexual feelings are an adaptation to unmet emotional developmental needs and relational trauma that occurred during childhood. If homosexual feelings are, as I contend, not genetic or a natural part of our design, but arise instead because of unmet needs for male affirmation, approval and affection, which lead to gender-identity inferiority, then it stands to reason that changes in sexual feelings would be remarkably evident in our clients' lives. And that's exactly what happens in the offices of myself and my colleagues.

I wonder if you can imagine what a cathartic and fulfilling experience it is for a client to look up one day in therapy and express, "I don't feel sexual toward that guy. Man, this thing of experiencing my *own* manhood in my *own* body feels a lot better than sex with guys."

When clients express these unsolicited moments of clarity and joy, I know two things: homosexual feelings are not inborn, and those sexual feelings can change. Their new experiences match their understanding of "who they are" in the deepest sense, and they align with their faith traditions. When that happens, I know they have finally begun to resolve, through enlightenment, self-understanding and self-compassion, the crushing inferiority that they have felt for so many years.

## CASE STORY NO. 2: THE THIRTEENTH THERAPIST

Sometimes it takes years for the traumas underneath a man's homosexual feelings to emerge. There are plenty of reasons for this. Although the client may be motivated to work on his past experiences, he is also resistant to doing so. And sometimes the traumas that he experienced are so deep, so many and so hidden that it takes time for his mind and heart to be ready for emotional breakthroughs.

The therapist may also be part of the problem. He may be limited by his lack of training, or by his own personal needs. Sometimes it's just not a good fit between client and therapist.

When Gerald, a psychotherapist himself, contacted me nine years ago, he seemed very motivated, even doggedly determined to resolve his unwanted same-sex attractions. He had done his own research, and had already concluded that his homosexual feelings arose because of early trauma and not as an inborn trait. His tenacity was one of the strongest I've ever seen in a client.

Gerald came to my office with good prior insight into the trauma he had experienced in his family relationships. He grew up in the heart of one of London's middle-class neighborhoods. His father was a well-respected minister of the Church of England, and his mother came from a well-to-do family. His parents met at Cambridge and had three sons within the first four years of marriage. Gerald was the middle son. At the time he contacted me, he felt he had to get away from his parents; in fact, from most of his family. And so he moved to the United States.

Over the course of more than a year, he told me that his parents had had marriage difficulties ever since he could remember. He and his next oldest brother were very close in age, and he was told that when they were little, his father had taken his older brother as his favorite, and his mother took Gerald. This parental "taking of favorites" was the initial, unconscious foundation for an immense amount of trouble for my client.

If Gerald hadn't had a stubborn streak in his personality, he might have given up on his journey long ago. He experienced bullying from peers, was left with unfulfilled emotional needs in relation to both parents, and felt weak and defeated for most of his early life. All this he experienced within an alcoholic family system.

His mother would tell him how awful his father was, and she so thoroughly emotionally enmeshed with Gerald that he felt he had to "rescue" her at the expense of his own needs. In short, he became the parent.

Gerald's father was the kind of man whom everyone knew, but who somehow gave sage advice to others without emotionally connecting with his own son. He didn't know how to emotionally bond with Gerald because he had never experienced a deep connection with his own father.

"Getting the right answers" to a problem and just "smoothing things over" without an emotional connection was the only response the son ever got from his father. It was an empty and shallow relationship, lacking depth and any sharing of feeling. The family rule he learned in response to distress was always the same: the admonition to "just get over it." And all the while, his father would regularly move into alcoholic rages—the only circumstance in which the man's feelings truly came out—and his mother would seek Gerald's protection, while his siblings reacted primarily by repressing their feelings.

But Gerald, as the emotionally sensitive son, was traumatized, and from junior high on into college, he harbored a growing suspicion that he was becoming a homosexual.

At the same time, at school, Gerald was being rejected and bullied by his classmates. This trauma initiated what would become a relentless pattern of panic, rage and anxiety episodes.

When he was 17, he had the bravery to tell his parents that he was having severe doubts about his sexuality, and that he wanted to see a therapist. But his father insisted that there was nothing wrong with Gerald's sexuality and that he could "just get over" any homosexual issues he had by thinking through it, believing in himself and forgetting all about his worries and fears.

His parents tried to reassure him that he wasn't gay, since, as they reminded him, he also had feelings for girls and wanted to be married someday and have kids. But as a young man studying psychology, his undeniable homosexual attractions kept him searching for an explanation in some kind of repressed trauma. This his father could neither understand nor handle emotionally.

After all, it was just a "simple" issue.

In effect, no one was there for Gerald. He had a deep sense of shame for having these unwanted feelings. This was one of the worst cases of self-hatred I've ever seen.

This tormented young man proceeded to visit therapist after therapist over the years, but they either had no expertise in child development and sexuality issues, or they knew his sexuality did, in fact, have something to do with his relationship with his father and mother, but didn't know how to help him move forward. Most of these therapists ended up repeating the very same type of simplistic reasoning his father had expressed.

Also, several of these therapists would conduct a type of "comfort" treatment that some of us in the industry call "bunny therapy"—*i.e.*, giving the client endless reassurance, but no challenge. This approach resulted in no forward movement. The work of these therapists can be summed up as not much more than "fluff" phrases like, "Ohhhh . . . I understand, mmm-hmmm . . . ahhh…" —all expressed in soft tones, but ending with little insight, no confrontation and little more than simple empathy.

So Gerald didn't get what he needed from anyone. And yet, he wouldn't give up. He conducted his own research. He went to see even more therapists. He even found a well-known psychiatrist who finally agreed with him that his unmet needs for male affirmation, approval and affection in childhood had resulted in an unconscious attempt to get those childhood needs met via homosexual connection. But in the end, even this psychiatrist didn't know how to help him. The therapist knew the "why" of his problem, but not the "how" to actually help him. This was harder on Gerald because he was getting nearer the answers, but couldn't move ahead and actually make use of that tantalizing knowledge.

For years, and especially since the bullying in junior high, a crushing sense of panic and doom would invade Gerald's emotional life, and the only experience that would make him feel better was masturbating to gay porn. Yet he had known for a long time this was only an emotional "anesthetic" that didn't ultimately resolve the pain, trauma and unmet male needs that still remained deep within him.

Finally, Gerald tried one more time—the thirteenth time—because he had found a website of a therapist who had been working for years with same-sex attracted men; that was how he found my practice. I was trained under the instruction and guidance of Dr. Joseph Nicolosi, the originator of Reparative Therapy, and the author of *Reparative Therapy of Male Homosexuality,* and *Shame and Attachment Loss*.

Gerald expressed from the beginning that he couldn't believe that finally, he had found someone who not only knew the etiology of gender trauma and same-sex attraction, but who could help him work through these issues so that a shift in his unwanted feelings and self-esteem might occur. And so we began our work, and he began to have good breakthroughs almost immediately.

However, it took Gerald years to break out of the strait-jacket of shame and abandonment that had confined him since childhood. That is a common problem with many clients; they may emphatically believe in self-forgiveness, *but they live as though they do not*.

Sooner or later all these clients have to deal with this dichotomy. For years, just like Gerald, they get into the mindset that they should feel horrible about themselves *just for being tempted* by homosexual feelings! They are taught from a host of experiences that they are disgusting, inferior, unmanly, and should be ashamed because they have these longings. They hear this from their families, their peers, from society, and some churches. When one is shamed simply for having feelings, a shame-based mindset will secretly take over and become deeply entrenched.

Do you *want* to create a homosexual? Shame him for his homosexual attractions and tell him to "get over it." All his issues will just go underground, and it will become even less likely he'll ever be able to move beyond his same-sex attractions.

I always work within a client's own belief system. If the client's belief system is Christianity, I point out that Jesus Christ was tempted to do many things, but that can't mean that he was guilty for being tempted. If Christ was guilty, then we are all lost.

It's very hard at first for these clients to realize the depth of their distorted thinking. Gerald was unconsciously shaming himself so that he'd be able to resist the homoerotic porn and masturbation. But it didn't work, since suppressing these feelings only creates a years-long cycle of shoving the feelings down, only to have them later rise up like a volcano to lead him right back to porn.

As we saw, this client had never been affirmed in his male identity within the context of a safe, loving relationship. How could he believe in and love himself when he was so ashamed, so unfulfilled, and had no idea how it felt to be loved unconditionally? Early on in therapy, I almost insisted that Gerald have compassion on himself, but it took him years to really *live from this place* of self-compassion, because, ironically, he felt safe in his familiar shame trap.

My client made quite good progress over the first year of therapy.

In our sessions, he was able to emotionally access his wounds, which resulted in a healing kind of grief and the development of an assertive anger, all of which led to a consistent and natural decline in his homosexual feelings. This happened because he worked to feel and experience his emotionally authentic self.

He always showed insight and made behavioral choices that demonstrated what anyone would call "good progress" on all his issues. But I knew there was something not quite done, not yet quite working to its fullest.

Can you imagine the loneliness this man felt? He had never acted out with any man sexually, and only viewed gay porn sporadically, but hadn't yet reached the essence of his core issues. Getting Gerald to the place where he could let go of his prison of being "safe" in his shame, and actually *transform* into relying on his authentic self with compassion and wisdom, was the very last stone to overturn. And overturn it he did.

Over the last several months, he finally cleared enough of the trauma away that allowed him to separate a sexual urge from the need for male affirmation. He began to trust me because I listened compassionately and consistently treated him as a valuable man. I had always treated him with unconditional positive regard. Hence, he finally learned to trust himself in the deeper places of his mind.

As a result, Gerald is now more at peace. He is more confident and doesn't feel such a need to justify himself or to care too much what other people think of him. His occasional lapses into shame have begun to fall away. He feels compassion for himself because he knows his homosexual feelings were not of his own choosing, but were the result of major trauma experienced during his childhood.

His feelings are resolving not because he is repressing them, but because he's finally reaching his most confident and authentic self. And as a natural consequence (never a forced issue), Gerald is experiencing feelings for women and wants very much to be in love with and marry a woman someday.

My client is nearing the end of his need for therapy. His deep traumas, which have been an actual form of PTSD, are in the final stages of being cleared out.

My hope, then, is that readers of this book will begin to understand how the lack of need fulfillment from a father can so greatly distort a boy's identity. So many of my clients express this same deep ache, this hole in their hearts, and a downtrodden sense of loneliness out of which spring a host of compensatory responses, including homoerotic feelings. Same-sex eroticism serves as a kind of emotional and sensual "anesthetic" that hides the pain and fear of inferiority that lie behind their unwanted same-sex love needs.

Without authentic Reparative Therapy as originated by Joseph Nicolosi over the past twenty years, I would not have been successful in helping these clients. Dr. Nicolosi's work was the breakthrough.

## Addendum II

# Chapters by J. Nicolosi, Ph.D. in Published Anthologies

Nicolosi, Joseph (1993), "Psychotherapy Can Change Sexual Orientation," in *Homosexuality: Opposing Viewpoints.* D. Bender and B. Leone, Eds., San Diego: Greenhaven Press, pp.126-32.

Nicolosi, Joseph (1994), "What Does Science Teach About Homosexuality?" in *Caught in the Crossfire: Helping Christians Debate Homosexuality*, S. Geis and D. Messer, Eds., Nashville, TN: Abingdon Press, pp. 67-77.

Nicolosi, Joseph (1999), "The Gay Deception," in *Homosexuality and American Public Life*, edited by Christopher Wolfe. Dallas, TX: Spence.

## Articles by J. Nicolosi, Ph.D. in Peer-Reviewed Journals

Nicolosi, Joseph (1993), "Treatment of the non-gay homosexual man," *The Journal of Pastoral Counseling* 28, pp. 76-82.

Nicolosi, J., Byrd, A.D., Potts, R.W. (2000), "Retrospective self-reports of changes in homosexual orientation, a consumer survey of conversion therapy clients," *Psychological Reports*, 86, pp. 1071-88.

Nicolosi, J., Byrd, A.D., Potts, R.W. (2000), "Beliefs and practices of therapists who practice sexual reorientation psychotherapy," *Psychological Reports* 86, pp. 689-702.

Nicolosi, J. (2001), "A developmental model for effective treatment of male homosexuality: implications for pastoral counseling," *American J. of Pastoral Counseling* 3, No. 3/4, pp. 87-99.

Nicolosi, J. (2003), "Finally, Recognition of a Long-Neglected Population," *Archives of Sexual Behavior* 32, No, 5, pp. 445-47.

Nicolosi, J. (2001), "The removal of homosexuality from the psychiatric manual," *The Catholic Social Science Review* 6, *pp*. 71-7.

Nicolosi, J., Byrd, A.D., Potts, R.W. (2002), "A critique of Bem's 'Exotic Becomes Erotic' theory of sexual orientation development," *Psychological Reports* 90, pp. 931-46.

Nicolosi, J., Byrd, A.D., Potts, R.W. (2002), "A meta-analytic review of treatment of homosexuality," *Psychological Reports* 90, pp. 1139-52.

Byrd, A.D., Nicolosi, J. and Potts, R.W. (2008), "Clients' perceptions of how reorientation therapy and self-help can promote changes in sexual orientation," *Psychological Reports* 102, pp. 3-28.

www.ingramcontent.com/pod-product-compliance
Lightning Source LLC
Chambersburg PA
CBHW060946050426
42337CB00052B/1607

*9780997637380*